Real Luxury

Real Luxury

How luxury brands can create value for the long term

Misha Pinkhasov

and

Rachna Joshi Nair

palgrave
macmillan

First published 2014 by
PALGRAVE MACMILLAN

Palgrave Macmillan in the UK is an imprint of Macmillan Publishers Limited, registered in England, company number 785998, of Houndmills, Basingstoke, Hampshire RG21 6XS.

Palgrave Macmillan in the US is a division of St Martin's Press LLC, 175 Fifth Avenue, New York, NY 10010.

Palgrave Macmillan is the global academic imprint of the above companies and has companies and representatives throughout the world.

Palgrave® and Macmillan® are registered trademarks in the United States, the United Kingdom, Europe and other countries.

ISBN: 978–1–137–39556–6

This book is printed on paper suitable for recycling and made from fully managed and sustained forest sources. Logging, pulping and manufacturing processes are expected to conform to the environmental regulations of the country of origin.

A catalogue record for this book is available from the British Library.

A catalog record for this book is available from the Library of Congress.

Typeset by Aardvark Editorial Limited, Metfield, Suffolk.

To Uncle

Contents

List of figures and tables

Figures

Table

Introduction

Real luxury is about leadership. Before the word "luxury" became intricately linked to the word "brand," the makers of luxury were considered purveyors of fineness and quality. They were leaders in their respective product categories. They took a product or a skill and evolved it into the highest expression of its art. The clients for this ennoblement were leaders themselves: the kings, clerics, merchants, and celebrities who served as role models for the values and behaviors of their community. This dual dimension of leadership takes luxury beyond the aspiration of simple ownership and translates it into a fineness and quality of intentions and behavior. Luxury brands and luxury customers influence people to act in a certain way.

We wrote this book for two reasons. First, the economic crisis that began in 2008 made it painfully obvious that the world could not go on with business models that rely solely on growth and put financial gain ahead of all else. Second, luxury brands are in a unique position to help the world find solutions to this problem and forge new paths ahead. The benefits to luxury brands for seizing this opportunity are many. By being social leaders rather than simple manufacturers, they will create a more prosperous and faithful market for luxury products. But to realize these benefits, luxury brands must see themselves in a clear, new light to better understand their role in society and the important potential they hold, both for their own development and the greater good. Do they understand the leadership potential this opportunity presents? Or are they content to play it safe, follow and pander to the market?

We are often asked whether our specialty is branding, strategy, communications, or human resources. Everybody wants to pin us down to one area, one role. But they shortchange themselves. Our work is none of these because it is all of them together, and more: psychology, sociology, philosophy, political science, and economics. We are actors in and observers of the luxury world, with experience in the luxury business and public policy. Above all, we are lovers of luxury who want to see luxury (re)claim its cultural leadership for all the right reasons. So we wrote this book for luxury brand professionals, management students in general, and personal lovers of luxury, who wish to better understand the role of luxury brands in society and adapt their practices to changing attitudes. In it, we provide a method for luxury brands to create value shared by businesses, communities, and, especially, individuals.

We begin in Chapter 1 by tracing the evolutionary arc of luxury in parallel to the evolution of society in order to understand the broad influences that made luxury what it is today, and why luxury can and should bring about the solutions to the challenges we face. Chapter 2 provides an analysis of what luxury can capitalize on and what it must be careful of in seizing the opportunities for leadership in the current socioeconomic and technological environment, which we describe in Chapter 3. Chapter 4 explores the transformation of value-making processes from the past to the present and their trajectory for the future. It presents an argument in favor of "leaps of faith" and sets up the idea of creating holistic, 360-degree value. Continuing this reasoning, Chapter 5 is an in-depth examination of the methods that businesses use to reconcile their commercial imperatives with the need to benefit society.

Chapter 6, which is the heart of our approach, explains the mechanisms by which we can identify areas of value that are relevant to the brand and its stakeholders, taking a business from being self-focused to other-focused, and building the bridge between creating art and creating value. Next, it shows how shared value can be turned into corporate purpose, integrating it with the business process. Finally, it shows how to get the individual to buy into a shared value proposition of the brand, creating a corporate culture and grounding the brand reputation in its actions and operations. Recognizing the demand for business models, Chapter 7 argues against the "business case" as an outdated and inhibiting tool, and in favor of building a value model that can help a company take the necessary risks that lead to innovation. In conclusion, Chapter 8 spells out how the ideas presented in this book work and will apply to the business of luxury going forward.

But this book is not a "how to" guide; it is not a technical handbook that shows you how to get from point A to point B. Rather, it is a "why" guide, advocating that luxury brands must first ask themselves why they want to get from point A to point B. Because each brand has a different "why," so each brand must develop its own "how." The methods we offer are for establishing a luxury brand's relationship with the world around it, defining its identity and purpose, and aligning its business processes and communications in such a way as to ensure its consistency and relevance for the long term. These methods are not for luxury brands alone. Indeed, they can be applied by any brand with sufficient visibility and presence in the popular culture; any brand with emotional sway. We address this book to luxury brands because of the unique set of strengths and opportunities they have available to them, allowing them to set an example and assert leadership and authority to complement the creativity and desirability they so cherish.

1

A dilemma across time and culture

• Luxury is the transition of an object from a product to art. It is an essential element of human civilization, in that it both shapes and reflects our values.

• People's relationship with luxury has always been a volatile one – whether in its pursuit or its rejection – paralleling the struggle to reconcile our competing needs as individuals and members of society.

• Luxury must always be at the forefront of creativity and innovation in pursuing the highest standards for knowledge and behavior as much as for product quality and refinement.

Luxury has always posed something of a conundrum to mankind. On the one hand, we are drawn to it, entranced by the very idea of something beautiful, rare, and superfluous, and on the other, it worries us, makes us question our values and priorities. Throughout history, mankind has developed philosophies and mechanisms to harness the power of luxury: ethical and political frameworks that reconcile its superficial excess with the underlying emotions that constantly drive us in pursuit of luxury. This is because we associate luxury with more than material trappings. Luxury, in the abstract, represents wealth, sophistication, desirability, and influence. Luxury wields a soft power, one that leads by attraction rather than by intimidation. It makes people want to imitate it and those who possess it. For this reason, luxury is a powerful social force.

Luxury sets a high standard, and becomes a reference to which future generations look for inspiration and knowledge. Today's art museums are pageants of the luxury goods of previous eras. When an object is good, the result of skillful production, it serves its purpose and creates a practical value captured in the sales transaction. When an object is very good, when its manufacture is the result of education and innovation accumulated over generations, it transmits emotion and human connection, and becomes an heirloom. Its practical value is matched, even surpassed, by its sociological value. When an object is truly exceptional, it enters the realm of art. It remains priceless long after its practical use is gone, as a testament to the abilities and vision of an epoch. It is at this point that the object transcends its original purpose and enters museums, too important to be used. It serves as a marker of time and a source of inspiration. There is an endless litany of examples: portraits of kings, period clothes and furnished rooms, silver table services, holy vestments, funerary items, carriages, the list goes on and on. But we do not only have to pick on examples from the classics for something to live up to. We can look to our own times for that as well. In 2013, the Metropolitan Museum of Art in New York held a retrospective exhibition of punk. The Museum of Modern Art in New York constantly adds objects from the very recent past to its ongoing archive of civilization. Its collection includes the classic Gucci loafer, the Eames armchair, the Apple (Macintosh) computer, and Dieter Rams' toaster designed for Braun. These are design objects foremost, but they are also luxury objects in the quality of conception, design, materials, and execution that make them inherently rare. The combination makes them iconic, a status that cannot be pursued, but is conferred by time and posterity (Figure 1.1).

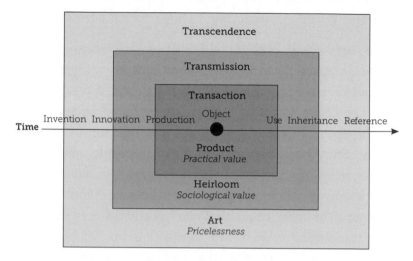

FIGURE 1.1 ╱ How luxury shapes culture

Right now, luxury, real luxury, is under threat. The industrialization of big luxury brands makes them act more and more like high-priced commodity goods with only a veneer of what makes luxury luxury. When you eradicate luxury, you lose knowledge and skills. Every revolution that has done away with the trappings of the overthrown elite has destroyed the knowledge of how to do certain things. "Russia" leather was an intricate technique of treating leather with the tar oil of white birches. But with the Russian Revolution, the technique was lost and nobody has been able to replicate it. Remember, though, that revolutions are not just political affairs. The whole theme of the last century and half was the Industrial Revolution. It was a persistent and calculated overthrow of old ways of doing things, of faster and cheaper methods of production. It brought huge benefits but has erased forever traditional and exquisite techniques. We lament the resulting loss of skills daily, from the scarcity of workers to restore historic monuments, to the more pedestrian lament of "they don't make things like they used to." We are suffering the loss of deep, intellectual reflection and insight.

The roots of today's attitudes to luxury

The ancient Greeks grappled with similar ideological dilemmas as we do today, that of political equality but economic inequality becoming increasingly pronounced. For ancient Athenians, luxury signified not just material possessions, but a leisurely pace of life, the time to reflect and relax.[1] This led to "sumptuous" inventions, such as chamber pots and bathtubs, which were then adapted by other cultures and found their way to modern times. But it also allowed the development of the arts, literature, architecture, not to mention philosophy and the first democracy. We can perhaps thank the luxury-loving classical Greeks for what we today consider civilization. Their cousins, the Sybarites, gradually became so obsessed with luxurious living that their name became, and has remained, a synonym for debauchery.[2] They banned cockerels from their city so as not to disturb their rest, they awarded prizes for cookery, and taught cavalry horses to dance to the flute. They also despised any form of labor, took along their lapdogs to the gymnasium, and their chamber pots to dinner parties.[3] This decadence ultimately led to their downfall.

In contrast to Athens and Sybaris, Sparta renounced luxury for a warlike state, with a lifestyle that can best be described as, well, spartan. In this context, luxury was seen as an emasculating and degenerative influence. However, even in this austere way of life, the goal of dying a hero's death on the battlefield was seen as a luxury that allowed the leisure class to devote their life to developing the body in the gymnasium and the mind in the political arena. Children were tested for physical fitness from infancy. Boys were trained in warfare from the age of 7, living in dormitories until they were 30, and were expected to be ready to go into battle until the age of 60.[4] Women, too, were encouraged to participate in sports alongside men. Compared to Athenian women, the Spartans had more freedom and were encouraged to run their estates in the absence of men engaged in war. War was considered a holiday by the Spartans, a relief from the rigors of daily military discipline.[5] This reverence of warriors meant that laboring on the land or engagement in crafts or arts was severely discouraged, and was relegated to Helots, or state-owned slaves. The large population of Helots was a constant menace to the smaller "elite" Spartan population; the threat of uprisings was ever present and reinforced their support of the military way of life.[6]

Especially after the Peloponnesian Wars and the ascendance of the Athenians, but even before then, the Spartan way of life gradually turned to activities of pleasure and entertainment. Military training was focused largely on athletics, javelin throwing, wrestling, and boxing. Very little effort was expended on weapons training, tactics or formations, as would be the case in modern militaries. For the Greeks, physical exercise was seen as a leisure pursuit and included hunting, dancing, and music. We can see here the seeds of what came to be considered fitting pastimes for the upper classes in later societies, and are indeed considered leisure activities, even luxuries, today. We can certainly trace our regard for fitness, health, youth, and wellbeing back to these origins.

The Roman Republic, inheritor of the Hellenistic way of living, had its own ambiguity regarding luxury. Between 182 BC and 18 BC, Roman lawmakers enacted a series of "sumptuary laws," restricting the number of guests at banquets, the number and nature of dishes served, as well as the silverware used.[7] Needless to say, these attempts were rarely successful; often they served to increase the perceived value of the forbidden goods. Some of the restrictions were specific to foreign wines and foods, which strikes a chord today when we think of protectionist measures taken by several governments, including taxation targeted at luxury goods.

While the traditional European approach to luxury was based on the need to create and maintain a social hierarchy, Confucianism had a different view. Scholars as far back as the Ming Dynasty in China have proposed that luxury consumption is not only beneficial to society, but also acts as a wealth transfer mechanism.[8] Ancient Chinese literature contains many examples of dynasties encouraging the rich to spend lavishly on tombs, coffins, and funerary shrouds in order to create work for craftspeople. The book *Kuan Tzu* (476–221 BC) advocates the carving of wood and making of exotic food in order to generate work for the poor. The writers believed that unequal wealth is the cause of unenforceable laws, since the rich are beyond the reach of the law and the poor are too poor to be afraid. Only when the people have full granaries and clothes to cover themselves will they be mindful of laws and courtesy, and distinguish between honor and shame. The Confucians believed that the amount of wealth in the world is fixed and needs to circulate, which is why they condemned "wasteful" luxury, or the dumping of wealth (goods or grains) into ditches. Confucianism criticized extreme frugality and extreme wealth, urging each man to spend according to his means in order to keep the economic balance. Thus, Confucians encouraged the consumption of luxury for pure pleasure, in sharp contrast to European attitudes, where luxury was equated with power and hierarchy. While aristocrats in Europe expected commoners to submit to their rank and position, in China, monarchs were instructed by Confucian teachings that the populace would submit for the expectation of the benefits brought to them. Even today, Confucianism is an underlying principle of economic policy in China and most of Southeast Asia, and still shapes attitudes to luxury spending and consumption.

In addition, the Asian self-view is more interdependent than independent, meaning that one's identity relies more on one's familial, cultural, social, and professional relationships than a sense of autonomous individualism.[9] Thus, the emphasis on harmonious relationships, group goals, and group representation. This, in turn, makes it legitimate to consume luxury without the guilt or embarrassment associated with it in Western societies, since it is a way of signaling not just one's personal position but that of one's entire group. The luxuries enjoyed by one member of a group are a source of pride to the other members, and not necessarily a cause for envy.

Indian tradition takes yet another approach. It provides a clear structure for balancing people's desire for the opulent with the fulfillment of a greater purpose in life. The four aims of life for a Hindu, known as "purusharthas," serve as points on a compass: they give meaning and help each individual to seek material and spiritual fulfillment. They are based on the philosophy that man is a microcosmic aspect of God, an objective personification of God's purpose. Similar to the way man makes an object or product as a reflection of his purpose, man as God's product reflects the purpose of God. Each individual is expected to pursue these objectives as part of the ritual of human life. The four aims, dharma (duty), artha (wealth), kama (desire), and moksha (liberation), encourage – indeed they oblige – the individual to pursue pleasure, but not at the expense of righteousness, and to always keep in mind that the ultimate goal of life is spiritual and physical liberation. The attitude one brings to the pursuit of these aims, including one's relationship with luxury, will determine if they set us free or entangle us deeper in their allure.

Industrialization and new dimensions of wealth

Until the Industrial Revolution, through the Dark Ages, the Renaissance, and the Enlightenment, socioeconomic systems, and thus the role of luxury, remained fairly constant. Before industrialization, economic growth was limited by the speed at which either nature or people could work. Machines allowed us to produce at a level well above that capacity. This new abundance opened the door to higher levels of economic growth and the creation of new wealth. Developments in manufacturing and transportation had the effect of turning erstwhile luxuries, such as cotton, indigo, and exotic spices, into commodities that raised the bar on what was considered to be luxurious. The advent of innovations, such as the steam engine, electricity, and the telegraph, helped connect the world of the privileged with travel and communications. Railroads and cables were laid. The *Orient Express* was introduced, making for easier, faster, and more luxurious travel between the imperial capitals of London, Paris, Vienna, Budapest, and Constantinople. Russian and British nobility began to spend their winters in the sunshine of the French Riviera. A network of luxury hotels, such as César Ritz's establishments in Paris, London, and Madrid, developed to receive these travelers with the latest comforts: electric lights, elevators, and individual bathrooms with hot and cold running water. Transatlantic travel – pioneered and epitomized by the luxurious ships of the Cunard Line, the French Line, and others – became much more advanced, with ever bigger, safer, faster vessels and more regular service.

This helped marry the new industrial fortunes of the US with the established aristocratic houses of Europe, creating the first truly global elite. Beyond Europe and the Americas, a global consensus emerged around the vocabulary of luxury, which was decidedly Western. Indian maharajas and Egyptian khedives began attending elite schools in England and France, adopting the tastes and habits of their peers in those countries. This opened up new opportunities for European luxury brands. From Jacques Cartier's trip to India in 1911, a long tradition grew of the house making jewelry for India's royal families. The client list of Savile Row tailors Henry Poole & Co. eventually encircled the globe from William Randolph Hearst in California, to Crown Prince Hirohito of Japan, via the Vanderbilts, Rothschilds, Isma'il Pasha, the shahs of Persia, and the Maharaja of Cooch Behar among many others.[10] The industrial advances emanating from the West created a desire by other cultures to appropriate this vision of modernity, be it technological or stylistic.

Through the first Industrial Revolution, from the mid-18th to the mid-19th centuries, luxury firms continued to produce as they had for generations, although they naturally took advantage of and benefited from improved transportation. While this opened up new sources and markets for luxury firms, it did not radically impact their way of functioning or their raison d'être. The second Industrial Revolution, from the mid- to late 19th century, however, had lasting impacts on luxury firms. Many prided themselves on their technological prowess and were at the forefront of adapting to the lifestyle changes taking place. For example, Louis Vuitton, Moynat, and other luxury trunk makers were among the first to start developing innovations, such as waterproof canvas, new mechanisms for locking and hinges, and light but rigid construction better adapted to new modes of travel. They used technological change to give a fresh impetus to their way of working. What did not change was their connection to a craft and skill set. Although they diversified their products, they did it with the same set of skills to which they had a direct connection. These firms were family run and consisted of members who worked with their hands, who knew their craft personally. This would not change until after the two world wars.

More deeply, the Industrial Revolutions also redefined what it meant to be elite, from an inherited status to one achieved through work. Prior to this period, most wealth had been connected to land ownership and rents. Industrialization allowed a rich commercial class to emerge among manufacturers and traders, and the bankers that financed their investments. These were the new clients for luxury. Its effects culminated in the Gilded Age at the turn of the 20th century, embodied by names like the Astors, Vanderbilts, Carnegies, and Rockefellers in the US. In a precursor to today's "Rich Lists," like the Forbes 400, New York high society in this period was identified as "Mrs. (Caroline) Astor's 400" – the number of guests that could fit in the ballroom at her home.[11] The name "Gilded Age" is itself quite telling. Notice that it is not "golden" but "gilded." The term was coined in the title of a novel by Mark Twain and Charles Dudley Warner, which commented on the visible layer of extreme wealth, hiding a slew of social problems developing underneath.[12]

Despite, or perhaps because of, the rise in privilege for some, attention also focused on the lack of it for many. The seeds had been planted almost a century before, when the Enlightenment brought forth new thinking about human rights and social equality. Well into the 18th century, as economist Bernard de Mandeville wrote, it was considered that: "To make the Society happy and People easy under the meanest Circumstances, it is requisite that great Numbers of them should be Ignorant as well as Poor."[13] In the late 1800s, socialism crystallized from a utopian vision into a political movement aimed at a more egalitarian society. An outgrowth of this vision also led to the feminist movement, fighting for women's property and voting rights, and equal standing before the law. The brewing social and political tensions eventually exploded into all-out war.

During World War I (1914–18), the machinery of industrialization provided the combatants with fearsome new weapons and a destructive capability never before seen. Aerial warfare, poisonous gasses, tanks and armored assault vehicles, submarines, and heavy artillery brought devastation on a vast and terrifying scale. Previous wars had been fought on battlefields removed from civilian populations, and certainly at a safe distance from the whereabouts of the sociopolitical elite. World War I was fought in the air and the cities, on and under the sea. And luxury was no safe haven, as the sinking of the *Lusitania* made clear. A luxurious transatlantic liner, the *Lusitania* was one of the icons of her time. The public parlayed her opulence, size, speed, and strength into proxies for her invincibility. But this iconic status also made the *Lusitania* a rich target for the enemy. She was sunk by another marvel of industrialization: the submarine. It made it clear that even the cosseted world of the wealthy was no longer inviolable.

The return from war accelerated the social shifts that had gone before: it strengthened the egalitarian urge. Men who had put their lives at risk for their country had little patience for inequality and the privileges enjoyed by the elites. The effect was to redefine and upend traditional notions of status and power. A spirit of rebelliousness took over. In design and the arts, new and challenging forms emerged, such as cubism, modernism, Art Deco, and the Bauhaus, which celebrated social and technological breakthroughs. Diaghilev and Stravinsky scandalized Parisian society with their cacophonic production of *The Rite of Spring*. Reflecting the strides made in women's rights, Madeleine Vionnet took scissors to the corset, while Coco Chanel appropriated the sailor's work shirt as a fashion statement.

The war also accelerated the technological advances that had come before, leading to even more powerful innovation and methods of production that could be applied to civilian life. Postwar reconstruction created a new economic boom and, despite the social pressures, continued to polarize wealth in society. This was the period of the Roaring Twenties, made famous by books like

The Great Gatsby and *Babbitt*, which explore the abandonment of morality in favor of materialism. At the dramatic culmination of *The Great Gatsby*, Nick Carraway, the narrator, observes of his friends:

> They were careless people, Tom and Daisy—they smashed up things and creatures and then retreated back into their money or their vast carelessness, or whatever it was that kept them together, and let other people clean up the mess they had made.[14]

A further development brought the burgeoning consumer culture into the public eye. This was the advent of motion pictures. For the first time, there was mass dissemination of stories and images, the creation of manufactured celebrities. These stories told both the fantasies and dark realities of this era. Charlie Chaplin's *Modern Times* relayed how mechanization swallowed up humanity. At the same time, Theda Bara and Rudolf Valentino became famous by bringing audiences exotic fables of wealth told in lavish cinematic productions. The effect of this new mass media was to reshape cultural values throughout society. While Chaplin's lovable "tramp" called attention to the underdog, the more potent visual was the dazzling and glamorous lifestyle of the wealthy.

Unsurprisingly, the Roaring Twenties were a boom period for luxury brands. The growing travel possibilities carried their renown far beyond their traditional home bases. Writer Dominique Lapierre estimates that during the interwar period, each Indian maharaja had an average of 3.5 Rolls-Royces.[15] In 1933, designer Henri Rapin, while serving as creative director for French trunk maker Moynat, also designed the Art Deco mansion of Prince Asaka in Meguro, Japan. Today, luxury brands love seizing on this period because of its rich aesthetic, its boundless optimism, and its sheer sensuality. The archives of houses like Chanel and Lalique are abundant with material from this era. But in their adulation of the hedonism of the 1920s, luxury brands focus on the object, not the spirit. In doing so, they forget that it was a flash of extravagance that ended in catastrophe. It was a period of financial speculation and the pursuit of lavish short-term wealth that turned out to be an illusion.

The 1929 Wall Street Crash, the Great Depression, and the war that followed would demonize luxury to a great extent. In 1931, heiress Barbara Hutton fled New York on a "European tour" to escape the public and media outcry in reaction to her extravagant debutante ball.[16] In times of mass privation, those with access to champagne, furs, even basics like meats and stockings were viewed with suspicion. Not only did such displays of wealth appear as clueless extravagance, they smacked of the abuse of power, of corruption, bootlegging, and illicit profiteering from the suffering of others. In 1932, the kidnapping of Charles Lindbergh Jr. and the deadly hunger march of Detroit's unemployed residents on Henry Ford's auto factory chanting "Tax the Rich and Feed the Poor" showed private wealth to be a dangerous liability. With the coming of World War II (1938–45), as the Nazis looted the wealth, art, and personal treasures of those they conquered, and as the rationing of necessities took over many countries, to have access to luxury goods was to have dealt with the devil. Luxury brands caught up in the maelstrom of this era had two options: cease operations or be tainted by blood.

Modernization and consumerism

The society that emerged from World War II was completely different from what had come before. The contrast was even more marked than the changes before and after World War I. Already suffering from the Great Depression, Europe and much of Asia were left mostly devastated by six years of fighting. The human toll was unprecedented. The atomic bomb dropped on Hiroshima killed 100,000 people in a single blow. The shock of the six million victims of the Holocaust would forever change perspectives on human rights. The world entered the postwar era bearing the emotional scars of 30 years of physical and financial struggle. The war effort also left us with massive industrial machinery and production capacity. The science and technology that had been developed to create tools of destruction would be turned to civilian uses. Combined with the physical and psychological needs of a healing world, this was to set the stage for the fastest acceleration in business processes and economic growth the world had ever known.

The beginnings of the postwar boom were in the need to rebuild Europe: to provision countries that had been obliterated by fighting with pretty much everything. In Europe and America, the machinery of war had kept many employed, either in the actual fighting or in manufacturing to serve military and civilian needs. In the meantime, populations had learned to do with less, as resources went to the war effort and households learned to ration and improvise.

With peace, the balance slowly started to shift. The world returned to abundance, and people focused on satisfying needs that had gone unmet for years. Once again, with continuing industrialization, many things previously available only to the upper classes or considered luxuries became commonplace. Goods such as cars and domestic appliances, and opportunities such as homeownership and travel became available to the average person. Even abstract notions, such as style and good design in clothing and interiors, stopped being the privileged domain of a few. This created a culture of prosperity and a self-reinforcing cycle in which the more we consumed, the more the economy grew. The generation born during and after the war did not know its privations first hand. They only knew a world of prosperity and growth. They would eventually rebel against the upbringing by parents who showed a greater caution in their consumption habits.

Their more basic needs met, people's desires and consumption turned more actively to the pursuit of comfort, pleasure, and aspiration. Without acute needs driving customers into stores, the relationship between consumer and producer became more subjective, more emotional. From the 1950s to the 1970s, companies evolved from a production and distribution orientation to one that emphasized sales and marketing.[17] With marketing, the focus turned to enticing the consumer to buy. This was the *Mad Men* era of dynamic, creative advertising executives who laid the foundations for modern brand communication. Desire, unlike need, is boundless. Addressing, and encouraged by, supply-side economic theory, production, rather than consumption, became the dominant economic driver, keeping people employed, prosperous, and consuming.

In the mid- to late 20th century, as wealth spread among the social classes, it became equated with happiness, which became equated with the pursuit of goods, and luxury goods in particular. The metaphysical qualities represented by a luxury good became less important and, in some cases, even vanished. What remained was the physical product, devoid of the higher purpose represented by the object. With the entry of financiers into a production-based model, value was no longer centered on need fulfillment. Needs, narrowly defined, had been met, so value became about how much profit could be made. To the financier, the higher purpose can have no place. The financier is looking for return on investment and the word "value" means the money generated.

Value can either mean material or monetary worth, or it can mean the principles and standards of behavior. In either case, value determines whether something is good or bad, desirable or undesirable. Value is a compass you use to chart a course toward your desired destination. Thus came a gradual shift in people's values, away from purpose and toward wealth, from "why" to "what." But as the purusharthas teach, desire is infinite and self-reinforcing. It can become an addiction unless we focus on the meaning behind the desire, the purpose of our consumption. When you know the purpose behind it, consumption not only gives pleasure, but also satiates desire and frees the individual to pursue higher goals.

In the West, consumerism had become something of a duty. With the expansion of communism, capitalist values provided a counterweight. Thus, material wellbeing became its own best argument against the gray and godless austerity of the Soviet Union. To buy was seen as good, as supporting the economy, as a fulfillment of one's patriotic duty, as morally righteous. The new medium of television rapidly entering people's homes reinforced this message, with shows that helped society luxuriate in the softness and pleasures of materialism, the comfort of the prosperous family gathered around the hearth.

Luxury brands, as we know them today, ripened in this boom and culture of prosperity. The postwar years saw the transformation of family-run houses into global brands. In the postwar expansion, established houses, like Chanel and Gucci, diversified their product lines and geographic presence, particularly focused on increasing wealth in the US and, soon after, Japan. New houses, such as Christian Dior and Pierre Cardin, joined their ranks, seeing opportunity in the taste for luxury after a decade of wartime hardship, and were quick to operate on an international scale. Three years after its founding, Christian Dior alone accounted for fully 5 percent of French export revenue.[18] Luxury houses also expanded licensing activities, with their brands appearing on an ever wider range of products.

Later in the century, this changed further still, with individual luxury houses coming together to form conglomerates. In this sense, they followed the example set by the rest of the corporate world as the deregulation of the 1970s and 80s led to a slew of mergers and acquisitions in the *Wall Street* era of stockbrokers and investment banks rising to prominence. As the scale of luxury houses increased, they needed the funds to invest in the expansion of their production and retail capacities. This opened luxury brands to outside investors. It should be noted that this was not a new phenomenon. Back in the 1920s, Coco Chanel had partnered with the Wertheimer brothers to finance her brand's expansion into fragrances with the launch of Chanel No. 5. What was new, however, was the much larger scale of these investments and the management and corporate culture they brought.

LVMH Moët Hennessy Louis Vuitton became the first such nonfamily-owned, luxury conglomerate. Long before Bernard Arnault, now chairman and CEO of LVMH, came on the scene, in 1971, Moët et Chandon merged with Jas Hennessy & Co. to become Moët Hennessy, consolidating the two firms' financial and market interests. In 1987, Moët Hennessy merged with the much smaller, still family-run Louis Vuitton. Henri Racamier, CEO of Louis Vuitton at the time, concerned about his brand's ability to hold its own in partnership with the much bigger wines and spirits group, invited Bernard Arnault, who had bought Christian Dior three years prior, to become a partner. This led to the establishment of LVMH, today the world's largest luxury group following the acquisition of numerous brands across the spectrum of product categories. LVMH now comprises traditional luxury purveyors, such as fashion, leather goods and accessories, watches and jewelry, wines and spirits, augmented by its ownership of yacht builders, hotels, and a worldwide retail and duty-free distribution network. LVMH is thus more than a luxury "maison" in the way that luxury firms used to be organized. It is in a position to provide a complete luxury experience, interfacing with luxury consumers at every facet of their lifestyle.

LVMH-style structure and management has set an example for other companies, even those still run by their founding families. The Armani brand is a multibillion-dollar global empire still in the hands of its namesake. Prada, while largely controlled by the Prada family, is also a publicly traded corporation, listed in Hong Kong. Even Hermès, the archetype of the centuries-old family-run firm, is a listed, public company, closely followed by bankers and financial analysts, and not just for their own Christmas shopping lists. French multinational group Kering (formerly PPR) evolved through acquisitions from a lumber company to a financial holding and finally to an apparel and accessories group centered on both luxury and sport/lifestyle, owning iconic names such as Gucci and Saint Laurent. Perhaps the most telling such arrangement is the group that controls Cartier, Van Cleef & Arpels, in addition to about a dozen other well-known, mostly watch and jewelry brands, under the name Compagnie Financière Richemont (known simply as Richemont) overtly revealing the investment impetus underlying its stewardship of such prestigious brands.

The queen is dead, long live Breguet!

We are a long, long way from the origins of luxury. "In the beginning" luxury was intertwined with two things: art and power. Makers of luxury goods were artisans at the peak of their craft and under the direct patronage of rule makers, be they kings or clerics. Their exalted status led to a pride in the craft that was innate to who they were and how they did their work. They signed their work as individuals, the precursors of today's brands. People looked to them for guidance about what to own, as they looked to the rule makers for how to act. If watchmaker Breguet gained acclaim because of the royal patronage of Marie Antoinette, this acclaim eventually caused customers to seek out

Breguet because he was Breguet. The brand thrives to this day, based partly on this heritage, but also because it continued to pursue its values, vision, and methods long after Marie Antoinette, even long after Abraham-Louis Breguet. Despite having to flee the populist reprisals of the French Revolution, Breguet remained in demand and was soon back in Paris to serve the imperial nobility surrounding Napoleon. Their endorsement was recognition of his skill and art. He provided a reciprocal endorsement of the means and taste befitting their status.

If in the past, royal patronage was an endorsement of the brand, today, it is the brand that gives the customer its endorsement. It signals the customer's belonging to a tribe. This is the aspirational power of luxury brands. But simple ownership of an object is a mirage that misleads the consumer and misrepresents the brand. It may be the symbol of status, but the reality of that status includes much more. The celebrity or leadership affiliation works both ways. On the one hand, the celebrity endorses the brand. There is an assumption that whatever the celebrity has is the best, and when making their own purchase decision, consumers will use that reference point to compensate for their own lack of knowledge and judgment. For example, when Kate Middleton married Prince William wearing an Alexander McQueen wedding gown, it led many other women to Alexander McQueen to buy their own wedding dresses. At the same time, armies of other women went online and to high-street retailers to buy copies of the exact gown worn by Kate Middleton. These women were not looking for the endorsement of the dress's quality. In many cases, the gowns they bought were far inferior. At best, it was an endorsement of the design, but really it was an emulation of the person who wore it. For a brief moment, a woman could be Kate Middleton, if only in her own mind. This is the raw aspirational power of luxury, even when it is inauthentic.

What, then, is the nature of leadership and what is its relationship to luxury? The combination of art and status gives us leadership. The status awes and the art inspires. But this leadership does not only belong to the leaders themselves. As we have said, it is a relationship of reciprocal endorsements. And in today's era of powerful, visible, global brands, there is an opportunity for the brands themselves to take on a role of leadership. Leadership is not something wielded with a stick. It is about inspiring people to follow. Neither is it the hypnosis of the pied piper. Seduction and glamour may have worked up until the turn of this century. But people are wiser now, and more skeptical. With the information age, people are able to see how companies work behind the scenes. Brands can no longer sell customers a pipe dream invented by marketers. Companies have become transparent, which kills the magic and mystery necessary for the allure and glamour on which luxury brands have come to depend.

Inspiring people to follow means providing an objective, a vision to achieve and from which to feel fulfilled. For many companies, their brand vision is "to be the leading ... ." But true vision is not a vision of yourself, it is a vision of the world you want to build. Luxury brands give customers a glimpse of a world that can become a part of their own vision. They do this by adhering to superlative standards. They represent the best that society can produce. And when they do this right, they become timeless. Not the marketing speak of "timeless elegance" but the reality of true timelessness.

But consumerism has denatured luxury. After a few flush years, when luxury companies felt they could do no wrong, their growth has begun to stagnate. This happened because luxury firms lost the sense of what luxury really is. Once rare and respected, luxury goods have become ubiquitous and meaningless; just another onslaught of stuff and advertising competing for our money and attention.

They became so obsessed with growing and marketing that they turned into panderers and stopped being leaders. It also diluted the perception of "luxury": when a thousand brands are clamoring for attention, all with interchangeable products, services, and imagery, where is the luxury?

Companies like Hermès, Louis Vuitton, and Cartier remained family firms for a long time. From generation to generation, there was continuity. After World War II, the control of these family firms passed into the hands of professional management, businesspeople who were not steeped in the company's essential craft. This led to exponential growth, but a loss of purpose. For example, in winemaking, one may love the product, but winemakers must also have a feeling for the land and the vines. The land thinks in terms of generations, not in terms of quarters. So can professional managers keep safe the brand's purpose, driven by what the "land" can do, or are they prisoners of short-term thinking to satisfy the market today? The maker knows the purpose of his goods, but does the financier? And does he even care?

Industrialized societies have increasingly valued growth and speed over durability and longevity. Now, in the information age, we are witnessing the limits of this economic model. But while sustainability and social responsibility have become popular buzzwords, the imperatives of technology and financial markets – and their promise of fast, easy gratification – prove difficult to resist.

By moving from an artisanal to an industrial model, luxury firms have exposed themselves to these same market forces that favor short-term thinking. Yet luxury is an inherently time-bound process. Its achievement requires thought and skill that are perfected over generations. The experience of luxury is heightened by the recipient's anticipation of the response to a long-term desire. The conscious recognition of luxury relies on its ability to "stop time," allowing the user to appreciate it fully in the moment, but also in the long term, sometimes over generations. Also, luxury's production standards lengthen an object's life cycle beyond its practical usefulness to become a sentimental and cultural reference point. Seen this way, the investment of and return on time are the overarching characteristics of luxury.

Furthermore, luxury plays an important sociological role in its ability to generate desire. The universality of its appeal is based on the emphasis luxury places on quality, creativity, and innovation, which stem from the fulfillment of essential, high-level needs such as affiliation, esteem, and self-actualization. Luxury reflects the values of society's leaders, giving it importance as a symbolic benchmark for the rest of society. When leadership values change, so does the trajectory of social evolution. According to some sociopolitical theoreticians, the pursuit of luxury has been the main driver of civilization since ancient times. Similarly, today, through their access to influencers and the influence of their own visibility, luxury firms can lead individuals and communities in the formation of more reasoned and responsible practices. Luxury, rather than simple extravagance, can therefore be a positive social influence, serving as a countercurrent to herd dynamics and a rallying point from which to confront complex challenges.

A call to action

Luxury, as the summit of production, as the conduit for innovation, has to advance something. It must stir progress, not just provide material comfort or display social status. This has always been the role of luxury and today the need to fulfill that role is imperative.

We are talking about leadership. As Seth Godin, leadership and marketing guru, would tell you, there is no map to follow, there is only the destination.[19] This is especially true of luxury, which must always be at the forefront of creativity and innovation in raising the bar and pursuing the highest standards known to man. These are standards for knowledge and behavior as much as for product quality and refinement. In fact, it is knowledge and behavior that underlie and safeguard the other elements that define luxury.

In the search for solutions to any systemic problem, there is too much focus on economics and not enough on human psychology. After all, people design and build these systems. It is then people's behavior that makes them function or not. Economic theory has long been based on the stereotype of the "economic man," the rational decision maker. But people are not rational. Neurologists have mapped that information first enters the brain through the reptilian complex, which controls our need for security. It then passes through the limbic system, which controls emotional responses. Only lastly does it reach the neocortex, which is responsible for rational thought. People have fears and blind spots, desires, and ambitions, which must be addressed before rational arguments can be made. If business and political decisions do not take the psychology of people into account, no long-term solutions can ever be found.

For business to address these challenges, for luxury brands to lead the way, we need to think differently about business. We need to think differently about brands. We need to think differently about our work. We need to think differently about value. We need to think differently about money. And we need to think differently about luxury.

Notes

1   Van Wees, H. (2012) "Luxury, austerity and equality in ancient Greece." Lecture at UCL Faculty of Arts and Humanities, November.

2   Lane Fox, R. (2006) *The Classical World: An Epic History from Homer to Hadrian*. Basic Books.

3   Op. cit., Van Wees.

4   Op. cit., Van Wees.

5   Scott, M. (2013) *Guilty Pleasures*, Episode 1: *Ancient Greece*. BBC Four broadcast, September.

6   Sabin, P., Van Wees, H. and Whitby, M. (eds) (2008) *The Cambridge History of Greek and Roman Warfare*, vol. I: *Greece, the Hellenistic World and the Rise of Rome*. Cambridge University Press.

7   Dari-Mattiacci, G. and Plisecka, A. (2010) "Luxury in Ancient Rome: Scope, Timing and Enforcement of Sumptuary Laws." University of Amsterdam.

8   Peng, H.P. and Chang, M.C. (2012) "The foundations of Chinese attitudes towards advocating luxury spending." *The European Journal of the History of Economic Thought*, 19(5): 691–708.

9   Markus, H. and Kitayama, S. (1991) "Culture and the self: Implications for cognition, emotion and motivation." *Psychological Review*, 98(2): 224–53.

10 https://henrypoole.com/hall-of-fame.

11 Patterson, J. (2000) *The First Four Hundred: New York and the Gilded Age*. Rizzoli.

12 Twain, M. and Warner, C. (2007) *The Gilded Age*. Digireads.com.

13 Keely, B. (2013) "Poverty, then and now. Part 1. Rich man, poor man." *OECD Insights Blog*, September 20.

14 Fitzgerald, F.S. (1925) *The Great Gatsby*. Charles Scribner's Sons.

15 Lapierre, D. (2011) *Freedom at Midnight*. Vikas.

16 "What a Swell Party it was!" New York Social Diary, www.newyorksocialdiary.com/node/3603/print.

17 Adcock, D., Halborg, A. and Ross, R. (2001) *Marketing: Principles and Practice* (4th edn). Pearson Education.

18 Pederson, J.P. (2003) *International Directory of Company Histories*, vol. 49. St. James Press.

19 Godin, S. (2010) *Linchpin: Are You Indispensable?* Piatkus.

2

The strengths and weaknesses of luxury

• It is tempting to interpret the growth of luxury brands as a sign of their invincibility; luxury is in danger of being hypnotized by its own brilliance. But business is cyclical, so luxury must understand and address its weaknesses to prepare for continued success.

• While people will always be attracted to luxury, its very popularity risks making it trite, a victim of its own success. Glamour is not the road to value. Purpose and meaningful connections with and between people are the richness that customers crave.

• Luxury's real strength is its capacity for thought leadership based on its own status and its relationship with society's elites. Luxury can set the standard for what is desirable behavior.

"2011: Another great vintage for LMVH." "Excellent outlook for 2012." These were the headline quotes from Bernard Arnault, as LVMH, the world's biggest luxury group, released the company's annual results in early 2012.[1] It was a sentiment echoed by other major luxury players at the time, dismissing concerns about stubbornly high unemployment, a public finance crisis among the world's richest countries, fears for the future of the eurozone, and increasingly rancorous sociopolitical discourse. Indeed, their predictions for continued growth came true the following year. The past 20 years have seen luxury transformed by seemingly invincible growth. First, the consolidations of the 1990s fused cozy, privately owned firms into multibillion-dollar corporate groups and marketing superpowers. The three biggest, LVMH, Kering, and Richemont, together now control around 90 of the world's most prestigious brands and have combined market capitalization of over €130 billion. In recent years, despite the Great Recession of 2008, these groups continued to balloon with new acquisitions, with revenues seeing double-digit growth. LVMH's annual revenues have increased at well above 10 percent for most of the past decade, exceeding 20 percent and even 30 percent in some quarters and sectors.[2] Share prices of every group have at least tripled since the depths of early 2009, and quadrupled in the case of Hermès.

For the astute observer, however, alarms should be ringing through the champagne toasts. Any business analyst or economist, or any scientist for that matter, will tell you that growth on this scale eventually hits a limit. Hard. The property and Internet bubbles burst despite mass projections of endless, exponential growth. And myriad examples preceded those two.

The consolidation of luxury brands into larger firms and the subsequent expansion of their marketing and distribution were heralded as democratization during the past decade. But luxury now walks a fine line between the scarcity that results in exclusivity and the availability to feed the mass desire on which they have come to depend. Luxury brands claim that they are recession proof. But are they? Certainly, there will always be a global elite unaffected by economic upheaval. Even revolutions bring a new elite and a new crop of luxury customers. But their numbers are not big enough to support an industry now accustomed to boundless growth. Despite luxury brands' claims, luxury customers are not limited to the narrow world of high and ultra-high net worth individuals whom they like to stake as their home turf. For one thing, not all the top-level customers are independently wealthy. Their ranks include battalions of professionals who are well paid, but must still work to earn their keep. Beyond them, we also know that luxury brands' aspirational customers extend well below the top tiers. After all, this is why the labels of $250,000 couture gowns translate into $1,000 bags, $300 jeans, and $30 lipsticks, the volumes of which are much higher and thus the profit margins much richer. Luxury now relies on a broad customer pyramid driven by mass aspiration and a revenue base including those more exposed to economic uncertainty. The growth of corporate-style luxury brands, indeed their whole business model since the late 1990s, has been to reach ever more new and younger customers. Thus, the temptation is to pander to the market: to produce merchandise that is widely popular and cost-effective, if not entirely affordable.

How far can economies of scale go before luxury is no longer luxury? Tom Ford said: "The 'democratization of luxury' promoted by the large luxury brand conglomerates is without doubt the main force behind the vulgarization of most traditional luxury fashion brands."[3] Lest we forget, however, Tom Ford was one of the masterminds behind the Gucci turnaround in the 1990s, which arguably established the template for luxury brand rejuvenations and expansions. The continued prosperity of luxury brands depends on the survival of the notion of luxury itself – a notion that is being pushed to the limits by luxury's own growth and ubiquity. There has been a fundamental change in the meaning, role, and function of luxury. In these circumstances, how can luxury brands maintain what makes them unique? Figure 2.1 provides a SWOT analysis of the luxury sector.

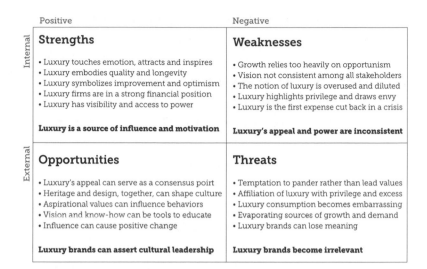

	Positive	Negative
Internal	**Strengths** • Luxury touches emotion, attracts and inspires • Luxury embodies quality and longevity • Luxury symbolizes improvement and optimism • Luxury firms are in a strong financial position • Luxury has visibility and access to power **Luxury is a source of influence and motivation**	**Weaknesses** • Growth relies too heavily on opportunism • Vision not consistent among all stakeholders • The notion of luxury is overused and diluted • Luxury highlights privilege and draws envy • Luxury is the first expense cut back in a crisis **Luxury's appeal and power are inconsistent**
External	**Opportunities** • Luxury's appeal can serve as a consensus point • Heritage and design, together, can shape culture • Aspirational values can influence behaviors • Vision and know-how can be tools to educate • Influence can cause positive change **Luxury brands can assert cultural leadership**	**Threats** • Temptation to pander rather than lead values • Affiliation of luxury with privilege and excess • Luxury consumption becomes embarrassing • Evaporating sources of growth and demand • Luxury brands can lose meaning **Luxury brands become irrelevant**

FIGURE 2.1 / SWOT analysis of the luxury sector

/ Illusions of grandeur

If luxury brands' revenues and share prices held up remarkably well in the economic malaise following the Great Recession, if they recovered quickly and stayed strong, so did those of other businesses. It was a flush run for large companies all around, as stock market indices returned to record heights even as the world economy only limped out of recession. So are luxury companies really special? Had banks not continued to give bonuses and golden parachutes even to their loss-making executives, had corporate profits and executive pay not quickly rebounded, had luxury companies not had territories of new wealth in emerging markets and the technology sector to conquer, had record oil prices not kept Qatari and Emirati money flowing into Harrods in London and the Four Seasons Hotel George V in Paris, would luxury brands have done so well? Luxury companies rode out the 2008–10 recession because of its unequal effects and a specific combination of circumstances. Beyond that, the record is mixed, where it even exists.

While luxury may be protected from acute economic crises, to conclude from that evidence that luxury is unsinkable is hubris. Just a year after the buoyant predictions of 2012, the headlines read: "Less is more for Louis Vuitton as it pulls expansion."[4] Louis Vuitton was not alone. Armani and Dolce & Gabbana closed their flagship stores on Shanghai's prestigious The Bund, after more than a decade of luxury brands treating the city as the new El Dorado.[5] At best, we can say that the market for luxury is still maturing. We cannot deduce any more than that. During the previous global recessions of 1998 and 2001, the luxury sector was in the early rounds of the consolidations that led to its current structure. Few of today's strongest luxury brands were publicly traded firms then or under the management of listed corporations. Most were still in the hands of the founding families and private investors. Their records are not available, and the investor shopping spree for luxury firms at the time would suggest that the companies they acquired were underperforming and ripe for a turnaround. A good run of a decade, even two, cannot be taken for granted.

As luxury companies have grown, they have had to rely on ever thinner markets. The 2008 crisis affected luxury's core market of rich countries most, where sales became volatile and any growth was fueled by continued success in a few narrow sectors. But new governance rules around executive pay, bank regulation, corporate and personal income taxes, banking secrecy, and so on put financial pressure on what luxury considers its customer base. While the still expanding emerging markets provided some compensation in the immediate aftermath of the crisis, even their long-term potential is in doubt. This has been most pronounced in China, the newest darling of luxury brands, whose consumers seemed to pick up anything with a prestigious logo. As China's growth began to slow in 2012 and 2013, Burberry was the first luxury brand to start issuing revenue warnings, followed soon after by Richemont, making luxury watchers nervous.[6] In India and Brazil, the opportunities proved more tepid. And mineral-dependent economies, like Russia and the Gulf states, proved themselves reliable only as long as commodity prices held up. Even as the US returned to more reliable growth in 2012 and 2013, and questions about the future of the eurozone abated, enormous doubt and uncertainty continued about the prospects for the kind of strong, worldwide recovery that luxury brands need to continue growing at the scale they had achieved.

If luxury really is to be recession proof, it must rise above the economic weather. Businesses that prosper regardless of external circumstances provide something essential. Witness the continued growth of the healthcare, energy, technology and telecommunications sectors through the darkest days of the recession. This is a challenge for luxury in particular, as the antonym of necessity. One luxury executive described luxury to us as "by definition, superfluous." Our question to her was whether she was content to treat her own work as superfluous. Everything that exists, exists for a reason. It must provide something essential, be it real or perceived, or the impatient march of time will eventually wash it away.

If luxury is content to consider itself – or to allow others to continue seeing it – as something superfluous, this prophecy will become self-fulfilling: luxury will seem increasingly bloated and extraneous and it will disappear. Or at least luxury as we know it today. In fact, it is already happening. Consumers are buying less luxury and being more discriminating about the kind of luxury they buy. Logo-laden products have seen the biggest decline in popularity and the brands associated with logos are falling from grace. This is sending luxury brands scurrying to respond with new narratives and new formats and forms of engagement to boost their sales. As the growth of luxury consumption slowed in Europe and the US, and as that contagion spreads to emerging markets, luxury companies' focus has been on finding new ways to push their transaction volume.

In 2013, Burberry unveiled a new flagship London store, where computer screens merged e-commerce with the in-store retail experience. Louis Vuitton launched Amble, a smartphone application with city guides, giving users the ability to share their travel photos and comments. Initiatives such as these get a bit of media buzz and their novelty value does draw some renewed consumer attention. But a retail or social media tactic is not the same as a brand strategy. Tactics are, by definition, time-bound, only valuable in their cumulative effect within a broader approach. In isolation, their novelty value dies down quickly because these are just gimmicks that lack any substantive contribution to the customer's life. The customer plays with these "innovations" for a while, before being left with a dangling sense of "OK, so now what?" They become fads, like the Angry Birds smartphone game, an entertaining distraction that enjoyed being a massive phenomenon for a year before being filed away in the back of our minds. But luxury is not in it for a year. Luxury brands identify heritage as being all-important. They do not go from season to season, but from generation to generation. Luxury's persistence in one form or another throughout human history shows that there is indeed something essential hidden under all that glitz. The challenge for luxury brands is to rediscover it.

Defining the undefinable

To really understand luxury, we must be clear about one thing: there is no such thing as a "luxury industry." This is not a philosophical observation about the incompatibility between luxury and industrial production. Rather, we mean that no such industry exists. Any good or service that exists in a luxury version also has mass-market equivalents. Fashion has Dior and Zara. Hospitality has Four Seasons and Motel 6. Cosmetics have Crème de la Mer and Maybelline. Automotive has Rolls-Royce and Kia. Watches have Rolex and Timex. You get the point: luxury goods and services are found across dozens of industries. Anything present in all these cannot, by definition, be an industry in itself. To talk about a "luxury industry" makes as little sense as to talk about a "low-calorie industry," a "high-speed industry," a "sustainability industry," or a "companies with red logos industry." The term "luxury industry" comes from the financial markets, which need a catchall that allows them to analyze and trade shares in a range of luxury companies as one easy-to-understand commodity. And a commodity is the one thing that luxury is not.

There is another problem word – "fashion." A large and very visible part of the luxury category, fashion's highly cyclical and celebrity-driven culture has come to dominate the image and attitude of luxury. But fashion and luxury adhere to different codes. Fashion is fast, seasonal, and obsessed with imagery. Luxury is deep, timeless, and obsessed with quality. Luxury is neither fashion nor an industry. While it is a product category, more importantly, it is the outcome of a particular vision and a certain way of working.

Luxury's essential nature is in its metaphysical qualities, not just its product or even its brand experience. Nobody buys a Cartier watch just to tell the time, in the same way that nobody buys a van Gogh painting just to look at sunflowers. Luxury attracts because it inspires and touches the emotions. In this sense, luxury is similar to art. Like art, luxury evokes responses we may not be entirely aware of. Like art, it has a tangible and an intangible component that carries different meaning for every individual. It holds a mirror to our perceptions of ourselves, our environment, our secret and not so secret desires and values. By embodying quality and longevity, it is also a symbol of optimism and a better future. It sets goals and standards for us to live up to, in our work and our personal habits. These are important, essential, psychological needs. And like art, luxury can even be an imitation of itself without losing credibility.

As long as somebody identifies it as luxury, it qualifies as luxury. This is where our personal relationship with luxury comes in, making it impossible to define objectively.

Because everybody's experience is different, definitions of luxury are notoriously hard to pin down. Luxury lies in the contrast to one's everyday experience and provides an antidote to workaday ills. One man's treasure is another man's trash. So, a factory or office worker may find luxury in treating themselves to a night at a full-service hotel, with gourmet food and high thread-count sheets. The antidote is in the freedom from chores, the opulent surroundings, and experiences orchestrated at a superlative level. A CEO might find that same setting mundane, even linked to a few too many business trips. The familiarity and association of something that is objectively luxurious nevertheless kills the specialness of the experience, even though the sensuous aspects can still be appreciated. Luxuryculture.com, an online magazine about luxury, profiles the designers, executives, and celebrities who populate the luxury world. Reading their interviews, a less material image of luxury emerges. Despite individual nuances and variations, the overwhelming theme is one of time: time to do a job right, time to reflect, time to spend with loved ones, even the existential race against the clock, to accomplish everything they want to in life before time inevitably runs out. For people surrounded by material luxury every day, be it their work or their way of life, the definition of luxury is much more abstract, much more philosophical. For them, the experience of luxury has to carry meaning that is at once beyond and expressed through the material incarnation.

At the same time, for management purposes, it is not enough to try and define luxury as something entirely abstract. That work is for philosophers and sociologists, although it is important for understanding luxury. To create luxury, you have to understand the abstract, but then you have to be able to translate it into the concrete. According to Diego Della Valle, CEO of leather goods firm Tod's:

> You cannot call something luxury because it is expensive. Luxury is something that is of high quality, very selected and produced by a company that works in a coherent way.[7]

In fact, luxury goes beyond even this characterization. We know that luxury functions differently from other product categories. The economist Thorstein Veblen explained it rather neatly in 1899.[8] In what is known as the "Veblen effect," a luxury good (or a Veblen good) operates contrary to commodities, in that their higher prices and lower availability, or rarity, actually drive demand. Often, lowering the price negatively impacts their desirability and status. A Veblen good is therefore often a positional good. Veblen seekers look for a distinguishing brand or product, to make themselves stand out from the crowd. When too many people start to carry that object or brand, the Veblen seeker moves on to something different or rarer. But this rarity goes beyond a simple question of supply and demand. Rarity of ingredients is a quantitative rarity. But the meaning that infuses a luxury brand is a qualitative rarity: only so many have the depth and vision to see it to fruition.

Luxury comes from the striving for excellence across design, craft, and production to create the ultimate product or to be brought to life in an experience. Luxury is to consumer products what the Olympic Games are to sport. When you achieve the topmost level of excellence in your sector, you become luxury. While Apple does not call itself "luxury," the brand is considered at the top of the information technology (IT) sector today. Apple have successfully used the codes of luxury in their branding, communications, and how they run their business. They set the direction and standard for the market and competition to follow. Companies look at what Apple are doing before figuring out how to do it cheaper.

Apple design their products around the experience they want users to have. They focus on the emotion. What follows in terms of technology, materials used, functionality, and look is a function of the emotional experience desired. This is exactly how luxury functions. Next come the obsessive attention to detail, the closed-end product, tightly controlled by the brand, and the consequent high pricing, all endemic to luxury. And, as happens in luxury, the higher price is not a barrier. In fact, as the success of the iPhone 5S and the flop of its affordable alternative, the 5C, demonstrate, the luxury customer wants and values the experience over the price, and even expects the price to be a gauge of value.[9]

Luxury's eroding value

The glamour of a luxury brand makes it attractive to all comers – consumers and employees alike. But when a luxury brand's employees aspire to carry its business card for the same reasons they carry its handbags, the brand has a serious problem. The contract between the brand and the individual is completely different in each case. Employees who come with the consumer's mindset, seeking to bask in a brand's reflected glory rather than bringing their own unique vision and value to the brand, cannot deliver the personal investment that generating luxury requires. This is true of any prestigious company, affiliation with which employees use as a badge of their self-worth. But for luxury companies, whose reputation is so heavily staked on desirability and perceived worth, this can be a particular peril.

Despite its roots in and constant talk of creativity and innovation, luxury today is a strangely conservative and passive business that actively avoids upsetting the status quo. Luxury's preferred vocabulary around heritage and its reliance on raiding brand archives to recycle ideas is inherently backward-looking. While designers may be willing to take artistic risks, while artisans may be willing to play with new techniques and materials, the army of merchandisers, marketers, buyers, and image makers need to be able to reassure their bosses and investors with products they know in advance will sell to a broad and therefore diluted customer base. The focus, then, is on playing it safe: mining a brand's existing image rather than projecting and propelling the brand into the future. You may get a new silhouette here and new fabric there, but this is not innovation of the sort that made luxury brands great to begin with. It is easy and therefore tempting to focus on the sale, rather than the more difficult questions of the brand's reason for doing what it does. Rather than being a tastemaker or leader, a luxury brand becomes obsessed with adapting itself to the lowest common denominator.

By taking its position for granted, luxury can fail to notice this eroding leadership and fall into the trap of working in a bubble. Originally inspired by and responding to a stimulus arising from the human condition, and a vision of how this condition could be improved, luxury has rapidly segregated itself. Luxury clambers into its ivory tower, raises the drawbridge and pretends it is all that exists in the world. Brands that think Russian luxury customers are ostentatious can fall into the pattern of assuming that they will always be so. Or that logo-obsessed Chinese customers will never change. But the customer does learn and evolve. Meanwhile, it is luxury brands that remain fixed, staring at their own reflection. Their knee-jerk reaction is to look for fresh pastures to conquer with the same techniques, where the customer is perceived to be as yet unsophisticated and hungry for the more obvious expressions of luxury. But how long before these markets too grow up and move away from a deliberate dumbing-down of the brand? Luxury brands must evolve with the times without becoming panderers, lest they lose their claim to timelessness.

People follow luxury and luxury brands for the same reason they follow those who possess them. Possession becomes a proxy for elite status. Luxury goods, by their association with role models, have become more than an aspiration, but a requisite for social validation. Many people now perceive ownership of luxury as a right akin to human dignity, and they feel deprived of that right when life's circumstances put luxury brands out of reach, fueling frustration and discontent. Philippe Khyr, the former publisher of *Elle Decoration* in France, says:

> Our parents' generation never felt they absolutely had to have a Hermès bag. Some people had them, some people didn't, and it was ok. Today, people cut other expenses and save for years to buy one. It's crazy.

Worse, it can be criminal. Sofia Coppola's 2013 movie, *The Bling Ring*, tells the true story of a band of Los Angeles teenagers, small-time thieves who break into celebrities' homes and pilfer brand name accessories.[10] It shows how the emulation of celebrity culture can quickly become an illness, with the possession of luxury brands as its symptom. On the one hand, the kids wanted a piece of their idols' lifestyles. On the other hand, facing closets crowded with handbags, watches, shoes, and sunglasses, they did not even think of themselves as stealing, so much as picking up overflowing crumbs. Material gain was not the point here. It was aspiration morphed into entitlement.

It should be no surprise, then, that the imitation of and black market trade in luxury goods is flourishing. This is not just a question of counterfeiting. Brands like Zara and H&M, and dozens of other legitimate firms in fashion, accessories, jewelry, home furnishings, and hospitality, have appropriated the look of luxury, even if they cannot match its feel or quality. Speaking to students at Sciences Po, one of France's top universities, Karl Lagerfeld noted: "In our time, you no longer need a fortune in order to be well dressed. This means luxury has to make superhuman efforts."[11] If the lawful challenge to their creativity were not enough, luxury brands must also contend with the never-ending threat posed by forgers, spies, thieves, and smugglers of their intellectual and physical property. Peddlers ambling along popular beaches or the avenues of the world's major cities are endlessly hawking fake versions of the most visible and visually imitable brands. One can find bazaar stalls and even entire boutiques selling what appear to be familiar luxury brands for pennies on the dollar. And, every few months it seems, the press is rife with news reports of an armed heist of Louis Vuitton shipments that disappear from trucks and airports.

This is the result of luxury companies' own hypertrophic marketing efforts to fuel growth following many firms' initial public stock offerings. Richemont was formed in 1988. LVMH, PPR, Hermès, and Ralph Lauren went public during the 1990s. Burberry listed in 2002. Ferragamo and Prada joined them as recently as 2011. Others, like Calvin Klein, are subsidiaries of larger public companies or, like Bally, belong to private equity firms beholden to institutional investors. Around them, a secondary industry of market analysts and pundits has developed. But, stock market imperatives of growth, efficiency, and squeezing performance and margins run counter to luxury's slow artistry and devotion to making something precious. There is a limit to which luxury can be multitasked, up-scaled, and distributed, beyond which it is no longer luxury. Superior, perhaps, but not luxury in the true sense of the word. Indeed, we are seeing the bottom layer of what has been called "luxury" cleave off into what marketers are referring to as "premium" and the hilarious but sadly unironic "masstige" – better than others in their sector, but neither rare nor precious enough to be luxury. To meet the demands of scale, in an age of global supply chains, luxury brands' efforts at strict control of intellectual property have not kept them from playing fast and loose with "Made in" labels, finishing products in France and Italy, while components and even assembly come from cheaper labor markets.

To many, the word "luxury" has itself become a cliché. Every new apartment tower in Manhattan bills itself as luxury based on now commonplace features like doormen, designer bath fixtures, and granite countertops. Cadbury have a line of "Luxury Cookies" available in supermarkets. Best of all, stop at a filling station outside France's Château de Vaux le Vicomte – luxury so extreme it raised the jealousies of Louis XIV, inspired the building of Versailles, and landed the royal finance minister in jail – and see the word "Luxury" staring at you in a curlicue font from the automatic hand dryer in the men's room (Figure 2.2). Old line luxury brands eschew the term, preferring to highlight the qualities associated with luxury. But this too creates a communications challenge. For some time, luxury brand stories have been converging around the same vocabulary – heritage, quality, craftsmanship, creativity, artistry, and exclusivity. While these words are all true, they have become an interchangeable and meaningless jargon.

FIGURE 2.2 / "Luxury" in a public restroom
Image © Misha Pinkhasov

To set themselves apart, luxury brands have turned to affiliations that illustrate their specialness. Art, with its high-brow intellectualism and jet-set clientele, was a natural place to start. Seizing on the obvious affinities, luxury brands have increasingly integrated art into their marketing. Events by watchmakers Hublot and Audemars Piguet and fashion brands like Fendi and Kenzo, not to mention yacht and car companies, have all appeared on the circuit of Miami's Art Basel fair. L'Oréal produced a commercial for their men's fragrance, L'Homme Libre, starring Benjamin Millepied, ballet dancer and choreographer and now director of dance at the Paris Opera Ballet, while Bon Duke's short film starred New York City Ballet's prima ballerina Janie Taylor showing off freedom of movement, dressed in fashion brand Chloé. Louis Vuitton cycle regularly through artistic collaborations on capsule collections and window displays with artists like Stephen Sprouse, Takashi Murakami, and Yayoi Kusama. But how often can brands do this before it becomes repetitive and thus highlights their dependence on others to provide artistic vision and content?

Going further, to establish credibility with younger and more diverse audiences, luxury brands have embraced pop culture through celebrity tie-ups. Sofia Coppola, who directed *The Bling Ring*, has designed bags for Louis Vuitton. In 2009, the brand worked with hip-hop star Kanye West on a line of sport shoes. In 2010, Kate Moss designed a line of bags for Longchamp, lent her tattoos as inspiration for a line of jewelry by Fred Paris, and her name to a take-out menu option at Sushi Shop. Celebrity endorsements are nothing new. However, they have become so frequent that genuine patronage by the stars – the equivalent of a royal warrant, the real aspirational value that the celebrity relationship provides – has become meaningless. It is one thing when a celebrity chooses a brand. It is quite another when a brand pays to be chosen. As journalist Vanessa Friedman points out: "these relationships have become so common and so public, that now when we see a star in pretty much anything branded, there is an assumption there's a contractual relationship there."[12] This is a particular problem because, of course, brands cannot control which celebrities buy their products or how they appear in the media. While Louis Vuitton may pay dearly for Sean Connery or Catherine Deneuve to appear in elegant, carefully crafted advertisements, the brand is likely less enthusiastic about a photograph going viral that shows boxer Floyd Mayweather Jr. sitting in a private jet, pulling fistfuls of cash out of his easily identifiable Louis Vuitton briefcase. Can the casual observer tell the difference?

Even supposedly safe affiliations can be tricky if they are not thought through. The 2013 production of *The Great Gatsby* featured clothes by Prada and Brooks Brothers, jewelry by Tiffany & Co., and Moët & Chandon champagne, and spawned collections, social media campaigns, and special promotions at New York's Plaza Hotel and elsewhere to convert these placements into sales. But in jumping on the Gatsby bandwagon, the brands seem to have missed the whole point of Fitzgerald's novel: a vicious impeachment of wealth and its corruption of moral values. Without even realizing it, the brands were mocking themselves, unable to look beyond the pretty things, so dazzled by the visual splendor that they missed the violent and tortured heart of the book. While the Gatsby movie was visually extravagant, it only served to reinforce the link between luxury and vapid excess.

This frantic effort to demonstrate relevance by affiliation is superficial, and thus fraught with peril. Luxury brands are conceived for the elite, but now marketed to the street. The democratization is meant to keep luxury fresh and hip, taking the edge off any hint of snobbery.

It is a fine strategy unless – and this is the important bit – brand managers lose sight of what it is that qualifies their brands as luxury.

When brands surrender to the lure of easy popularity, we begin to see the backlash of these tactics. Luxury brands begin to look like a beauty growing desperate with age. Once the El Dorado of anything-goes, logo-star-struck marketers, China's luxury consumers are wising up faster than expected and looking for deeper, more meaningful connections with brands and their products. If they do not find them, they will move on to brands that can provide them. In Russia, a massive Louis Vuitton installation was chased off Red Square just before the 2013 holiday shopping season after a public and politically motivated outcry at the ostentatious display.[13]

Superficiality reduces the status of luxury to bling, devoid of the vision, passion, and culture that contributed to its success in the first place. It subsumes luxury to the cult of celebrity, vanity, and greed. This can quickly make luxury embarrassing. Take, for example, the case of Robert Diamond, the former CEO of Barclays bank, who in 2011 called for bankers to "stop apologizing" for causing the crash and cited Barclays' record of upstanding behavior, while defending the payout of large bonuses before the UK's Treasury Select Committee.[14] Diamond stepped down from his position at Barclays a year later amid charges and fines for the bank's illegal manipulation of currency markets.[15] Three years prior, during the outset of the crisis, Diamond had apparently paid $37 million for a New York penthouse under the pseudonym of Novgorod.[16] It threw a red herring to luxury real estate watchers, who assumed that the buyer was yet another Russian oligarch. That a member of the respectable British banking establishment would feel the need to masquerade as a shady Russian arriviste to make a luxury purchase "blend in" speaks volumes about where perceptions of luxury consumption and luxury consumers are headed.

The flip side of luxury's visibility is that it can draw scrutiny, envy, and ire. When those in positions of power and privilege become so wrapped up in satiating the senses, they become soft and indifferent to the reality beyond their own. Social structures become top-heavy and inevitably weigh on the layers underneath. One of the triggers of the French Revolution was the hoarding of flour by the wealthy to powder their wigs while the poor starved. Although luxury may only be a symbol of deeper decay in such circumstances, it becomes associated with everything that has gone wrong with society and becomes entangled with its collapse. And while luxury brands are not responsible for the ills of society, they do become the targets of its wrath. In 2012, following a spate of scandals that caused popular anger over official corruption, the Chinese government issued rules limiting the value of official gifts. Luxury brands were banned from advertising on television and billboards because, as the State Administration of Radio, Film and Television said, such advertising "publicized incorrect values and helped create a bad social ethos."[17] Chinese luxury customers started to reject the more ostentatious brands, and erstwhile juggernaut brands had to contend with rapidly decreasing sales. Later in the year, on the other side of the world, a street art campaign saw the phrase "RESERVED FOR HOMELESS N52672" stenciled in an official-looking font near the entrances to the Chanel and Louis Vuitton boutiques, and elsewhere in New York's fashion-conscious SoHo neighborhood (Figure 2.3). The message behind these two very different efforts seems clear: to shame luxury customers and move them to a consciousness beyond simple conspicuous consumption.

FIGURE 2.3 / Chanel boutique in New York's SoHo neighborhood

Image © Frédéric Warnery

Finding gold beyond the glitter

Social harmony and stability rely less on an equal distribution of wealth than on an equal distribution of a feeling of dignity and self-worth. When people stake their self-worth on the ownership of luxury objects, this gives makers of luxury goods a responsibility they may not have volunteered for, but which they are nonetheless encumbered with and to which they must respond. If they ignore this responsibility by feeding the frenzy for luxury, especially in an environment where society is becoming increasingly polarized, they risk hollowing out their own meaning and relevance, and stirring resentment. Or they can seize the opportunity for leadership by directing the mass desire towards an understanding of value beyond materialism. One can appreciate and learn from a work of art about beauty, about people, and about life without having to possess the object. Luxury, as an art form applied to the realm of products, can educate people about the metaphysical aspects of consumerism. The antidotal quality of luxury – the characteristics that make it feel "right" – can educate people about shortcomings elsewhere.

For example, the accelerating consumer culture is blamed for a wide range of problems from natural resource depletion to pollution, waste, and household indebtedness. The pressure to keep up, as a consumer and a business, is a major cause of social breakdown due to increased anxiety, stress, and poor work–life balance. And yet, all this consumption, driven by a culture of instant gratification, has not led to higher levels of personal satisfaction. Luxury is a counterweight to meaningless consumption. Luxury's value is anchored in the backstory to the product; a backstory based on time, knowledge, expertise, and passion. When the LVMH brands – couturiers, wineries, watchmakers, and others – throw open their doors to the public during the *Journées Particulières*, they use this backstory to instill respect for how the object comes into being. When Chanel display their No. 5 fragrance in the context of modernist art and Bauhaus design in which it was created, it illustrates how perfume is not just ornamental, but can be part of society's intellectual and cultural evolution.[18] This depth gives it its timelessness. Thus, luxury teaches people what to look for, and provides an alternative to instant gratification by deploying the even greater pleasures of anticipation and long-term relevance. Luxury becomes a celebration of self-worth rather than a precondition to self-worth.

Luxury has power. In a simplistic way, this is because luxury has long addressed itself to those who lead. More importantly, it is because of luxury's ability to influence our behavior. Luxury has a privileged relationship with individuals who have the means, connections, and authority to change entire systems. Since our most ancient civilizations, luxury has been the domain of those in positions of influence, whether political, religious, economic, or social. Historically, there were formal restrictions on the wearing of certain fabrics, the eating of certain foods, the ownership of precious metals, and access to certain types of knowledge or education to specific social categories. For example, in medieval Europe, purple was a color worn only by royalty, as yellow was in China. In Aztec culture, meat and fish were foods reserved for the elite, while peasants ate mostly greens and grains.[19] In cultures the world over, education was long controlled by religious institutions and only available to the sons of noble families. With time, these laws softened into social custom, protected instead by the economic barrier to being able to access them. These symbols and behaviors then opened up to those who desire to mimic the customs of the privileged. In this way, luxury has long been the symbol not just of privilege, but of access and power. This is partly what makes luxury goods and brands desirable. Their possession and their visibility serve as signals of one's position, as an objective to strive towards, and a behavior to emulate: the markers of one's status.

Luxury used to be a humble profession. Skilled artisans worked in the shadow of the kings they served. Unlike the designers and CEOs of today, who compete with celebrities and socialites on magazines' people pages, they were the backstage laborers who helped others put on a dazzling performance. Their acclaim came from the quiet reverence of insiders, reserved for experts and masters of skills that seem like magic to the rest of us. This ability to make magic is the result of years of meticulous preparation and training that – like

Olympic athletes, surgeons, or astronauts – put their skills beyond the reach of those without the obsessive devotion necessary to become the best and that continue to be honed and improved even after fame has been achieved.

This deep expertise, this obsession with detail, and this devotion to the craft allowed luxury to be a conduit for innovation. The early adopters of innovation are those who can afford to explore the boundaries of the possible before it becomes accessible to us all. Paper was first developed in China as a luxury only available to a privileged few. Yet, the development of paper paved an easier way to the dissemination of knowledge than did its predecessors, such as woven fabrics, vellum, and parchment, or carved stone and bronze. New materials and techniques were taken up by luxury not just because they were novel or even rare, but because they had a functional advantage that allowed the product to perform at ever higher levels. Similarly, travel trunks, now icons of luxury from brands like Louis Vuitton, Goyard, and Moynat, evolved from heavy, furniture-like wooden chests to much more practical and agile cases of lighter construction. The natural properties of leather were used to insulate the contents from the weather. In 1854, Moynat began to replace leather with even lighter canvas coated in gutta-percha, a derivative of natural latex. This revolutionized the trunk-making industry as other houses adopted similar practices. Note that these innovations were driven by performance criteria. The objective was to produce goods for those who could afford the best, whatever the cost. Hermès earned their reputation by being the best in class among saddlers. They eventually extended this approach, first to other equestrian accessories, then to leather goods more generally, and finally to a whole range of fashion and home goods, ranging from silk scarves to entire custom interiors. The emphasis is on useful and beautiful products that are exquisitely made. Whatever it is you are looking for, you can be sure to find the finest at Hermès.

Throughout time, the desire and demand for luxury has pushed the boundaries of our way of living even for those outside the elite. From indoor plumbing to electric lighting, telephones, automobiles, appliances, air travel, televisions, home computers, and mobile phones, all these inventions were accessible only to a privileged few. To begin with, not only was each of these innovations expensive, but also superfluous, often frightening and even perilous. One had to have not only the financial means, but also the appetite for risk. Yet, it was precisely this seduction and bravado that created allure and generated demand. In turn, these innovations proved their practical usefulness and developed the economies of scale that eventually made erstwhile luxuries accessible, even indispensable, to the masses.

Today, the notion of luxury continues to push standards of performance, comfort, and ease. Airlines introduce new concepts and comforts in first and business class before rolling some of them out to the back of the plane. Motor racing, long seen as a rich man's pursuit, has yielded most of the innovations found in vehicles on the roads today. Similarly, hybrid and electric cars are priced higher than their gas-guzzling counterparts. The most promising – Tesla, Toyota's Prius, and BMW's i series – appeal to the same customers who buy luxury brands, and have learned that they must speak these customers' language in terms of design, feel, features, and performance.

If luxury is to maintain the delicate balance between being aspirational and yet omnipresent, extravagant and yet revered, it should not seek to follow the prevailing consumer culture, but to lead it. That means rediscovering the depth and intellect that made luxury brands what they are. Glamour and celebrity are integral to luxury's image, but luxury should not use them as a replacement for its own substance.

When Marilyn Monroe famously said in an interview that she only wore Chanel No. 5 to bed, that was the star choosing the brand.

You cannot buy that kind of publicity because it is unplanned, spontaneous, and authentic. And the story has remained alive in the collective memory for decades after it happened, becoming a part of the legendary personality and the legendary brand. However, if we focus only on the celebrity link, we are just seeing the most obvious tip of the iceberg. We miss the tremendous backstory that allowed it to happen at all.

Until the early 1920s, most women's perfumes fell into one of two categories. Perfumes that evoked the scent of a single flower were for proper ladies, while more provocative, musky, and heavy perfumes signified a woman of more dubious virtues. In her choice of fragrance, a woman was confined to these two extremes of social approval or opprobrium. There was no place in the world for a woman who was an upstanding member of society, but in touch with her physical needs and sensuality. The mere suggestion of the sexual nature of a woman was an invitation for scandal. Gabrielle (Coco) Chanel, in keeping with her ethic and personality, wanted to create a perfume to represent the liberated woman of the 1920s, one who did not have to choose between being "pure" or a "prostitute." The perfume she created is a composite of many floral notes, unidentifiable as any single flower, and unabashedly synthesized, without pretensions of being natural. It is an abstraction of a bouquet of flowers. According to Jacques Polge, the "nose" of the House of Chanel, it would evoke quite simply the smell of a woman, "perfectly balanced between a presence and a mystery."[20]

In that abstraction, Chanel No. 5 was part of the major artistic, creative, and philosophical shifts at the time, which were revolutionizing traditional lifestyles with a bold modernism. The cubism of Picasso and Braque, the surrealism of Dali, and the dadaism of Duchamp were shaking up representational art. Architecture was being transformed by Art Deco and the Bauhaus. The abstraction achieved by Chanel No. 5 meant that the perfume was literally multifaceted, like the essential nature of a woman: complex and comprising many parts, all of which converge to form a greater whole. This, then, is the real connection between Chanel No. 5 and Marilyn Monroe, the woman who represented the multifaceted nature of women: part innocence, part sensuality, a presence and a mystery all at once.

So Chanel No. 5 was no simple brand extension. It was the extension of a vision, a reaction to the world and a marriage with the forward-thinking movements of the period. Questions about what makes a woman free to be and to express herself, what makes her desirable in her own eyes are as relevant today as they were in the 1920s. And so Chanel No. 5 has retained its appeal over time, meaning many different things to many different women. Even the bottle has remained perfectly in tune with contemporary design sensibilities. Its minimalist, almost masculine lines put forward the contents rather than the container, an echo of Coco Chanel's approach to clothing. Its deep roots and intellectual approach ensure its timelessness, in the same way that the roots and intellect of art allow it to remain relevant and instructive for centuries.

Like art, luxury has the ability to act on our behaviors and influence, or at least reflect on, our values. It opens the door to different ways of thinking and acting. Luxury has the added effect of making them desirable to emulate.

While the public may focus on the products and the glamour of luxury, the brands themselves cannot afford to ignore or underestimate the importance of the submerged part of the iceberg, which will determine the impact of the whole. When they do so, not only do they abdicate the responsibility of wise leadership that comes with the territory of status, but they also turn their backs on the opportunities for carving a unique and inimitable niche for themselves in the market. Worse, they voluntarily give up control of their brand's voice, its power to shape its universe. When the managers of a luxury brand cannot see beyond the product and its quarterly sales, they are in effect handing over the living heart of the brand to the lowest bidder: all the intangibles that make up its value system, its point of view, and the consistency that leads to its customers' trust. And this, once lost, is difficult to rebuild.

Notes

1   LVMH press release (2012) "2011: Another great vintage for LVMH." February 2. www.lvmh.com/press/621.

2   LVMH Annual Reports 2008–2013.

3   Hunt, P. (2012) "The geography of pricing luxury brands online." *Financial Post*, September 2.

4   Reuters (2013) "Less is more for Louis Vuitton as it pulls expansion." February 1.

5   *Want China Times* (2014) "Sales of luxury goods decline substantially in China." January 7.

6   Jolly, D. (2012) "Burberry warns of weakness in luxury market." *The New York Times*, September 11.

7   www.luxuryculture.com/luxury-now/diego_della_valle.

8   Veblen, T. ([1899]1994) *The Theory of the Leisure Class: An Economic Study of Institutions*. Dover.

9   Gross, D. (2013) "Is Apple's iPhone 5C a flop?" CNN, international edition, October 18.

10   Coppola, S. (dir.) (2010) *The Bling Ring*. Based on Sales, N.J. (2010) "The Suspects Wore Louboutins." *Vanity Fair*, March.

11   Agence France-Presse (2013) "Karl Lagerfeld à Sciences Po: 'Coco Chanel m'aurait détesté'." *Le Huffington Post*, November 20.

12   Friedman, V. (2013) "An unexpected problem with celebrity endorsement." *Financial Times*, January 23.

13   Moh, C. (2013) "Giant Louis Vuitton suitcase to leave Moscow's Red Square." BBC News Europe, November 28.

14   Kirkup, J. (2011) "Bob Diamond: Bankers should stop apologizing." *The Telegraph*, January 11.

15   Schaefer Muñoz, S. and Colchester, M. (2012) "Top Officials at Barclays Resign Over Rate Scandal." *The Wall Street Journal*, July 4.

16   Velsey, K. (2013) "Guess Where Barclays' Disgraced CEO Bob Diamond Spent His Ill-gotten Gains?" *New York Observer*, January 14.

17 VOA News (2013) "China bans ads for luxury goods." *Voice of America.* February 6.

18 Prodhon, F. (2013) *No. 5 Culture Chanel,* exhibition guide. Chanel.

19 Coe, M. and Koontz, R. (2002) *Mexico: From the Olmecs to the Aztecs.* Thames & Hudson.

20 Interview with Jacques Polge. "Chanel No. 5: Story of an Icon," www.youtube.com/watch?v=zXjk8G-K3lI. Accessed 3/6/14.

3

The environment
for luxury

- People have a new awareness of the shortcomings of long accepted business practices and objectives. This disillusionment causes a breakdown of trust, revolutionizes our ways of thinking, and influences our choices as citizens and consumers.

- While people's desire for luxury is unchanged, it is finding forms of expression that combine personal pleasure with a positive impact in the world.

- Luxury brands that want to be seen as leaders must find ways to transform visceral wants into civilized desires, so that we can both indulge and manage our appetites.

Luxury is a reaction to the world around it. Its rarity is not in the simple lack of supply. It is in the contrast luxury provides to one's everyday experience. Luxury soothes and reassures body, mind, and spirit. Like an antidote, luxury distinguishes itself by providing an uncommon, better alternative to the present. So, understanding luxury also means understanding people's lives. It is not enough to understand your product. You have to understand how people integrate it into their thought processes. It is not enough to understand your market. You have to understand the dynamics in the community. It is not enough to be a manager. You have to be part psychologist, part sociologist, part economist, part political scientist, and part philosopher. You have to gather evidence from all these fields in order to make an analysis and come to a conclusion. You have to take the broad and the long view, a weakness of most management practice, which focuses on the immediate.

Short-term phenomena – economic cycles, shopping habits, consumer trends – are signs of bigger forces, like people's perceptions of security, fair play, access to opportunity, their wellbeing, their future prospects, and their values. These forces are important to understand if you want to predict and respond to rapidly evolving market conditions effectively. Managers today are pressed to respond to the symptoms right now, not the root causes. But if we race around focusing on only the surface signals, we can misunderstand what is really happening and be caught unprepared for what will happen next. A macro-vision that can ride out fluctuations is crucial to building enduring strategies and long-term brands.

Frédéric Oudéa, CEO of Société Générale, the French banking giant, described the bank's lessons from a series of crises beginning in 2008:

> It became very clear to me that we at Société Générale needed a long-term vision that would remain unchanged, regardless of what happened around us – the Euro Zone crisis, volatility in the markets, changing regulations, political risk. I wanted to align us with a long-term vision that would make sense in any circumstance and make our people proud to be bankers.[1]

The macro-currents running through society today are remarkably unchanged since industrialization. History shows us a consistent and discernable pattern. Technology is the first domino that sets off a chain reaction of worldwide economic, social, and, finally, political change. It gives rise to new means of production and communication. It creates new products and consumer habits. It connects cultures and ideas from around the world. It redistributes wealth and power. It changes value systems. It evolves thinking about social structures. It upsets existing hierarchies. It dismantles old establishments and erects new ones. With each cycle of technological innovation, we have been moving away from submitting to institutions towards empowering individuals; from pursuing wealth to pursuing wellbeing; from satisfying needs to fulfilling ambitions. This pushes notions of luxury in new and more nuanced directions.

	Normative	Objective
Forces	**Political** • Scramble to manage the crisis "domino effect" • Few consensus ideas about the way forward • Increasing regulation of business conduct • Vested interest groups blocking reform efforts • Lack of pragmatic and trusted leading figures **A need for innovation and integrity**	**Economic** • Ongoing uncertainty and instability • Fewer sure vales and sources of growth • Cost-cutting reorders spending priorities • Unemployment and austerity taking social toll • Indicators that the crisis will change shape **A need for substance and reliability**
Trends	**Societal** • Growing fear and mistrust about the future • Perception of an unfairly privileged minority • Crisis of confidence in "The Establishment" • More emphasis on individual rights and voice • Institutions and elites called to responsibility **A need fo trust and solidarity**	**Technological** • Explosion of new sources of information • More channels for exchanging ideas • Greater transparency of institutions • Speed increases competitive pressures • More complexity in control of messages **A need for sincerity and engagement**

FIGURE 3.1 / PEST analysis of the environment for luxury brands

Luxury brands' success depends on notions of status and aspiration. Evolving definitions of success and new notions about status and leadership mean that the affiliations on which luxury has long relied are carrying less weight and having less influence. By toeing the same familiar line, luxury brands risk falling increasingly out of step with the times. Luxury brands today have come to depend on tactics that highlight luxury's glamour rather than its relevance.

Glamour is hypnotic and numbing, but an anesthetic is not an antidote. Until luxury brands reenvision and reposition themselves as purveyors of something other than extravagance, they are putting their reputations at risk. Figure 3.1 above provides an analysis of the political, economic, societal, and technological (PEST) environments for luxury brands.

The prosperity trap

When we speak with luxury brand executives, they say they want to have a positive impact on the world. Despite appearances, they are not content to just build commercial empires, but want to create a legacy. Luxury brands contribute to philanthropic causes, preserve national cultural heritage, and support the arts. They are also aiming to make their companies more socially responsible and sustainable by helping to preserve employment in traditional craftsmanship, provide quality products, and improve their environmental practices. But then they tell us that they need to be able to justify these efforts in their quarterly results and rapid growth, and that the customer demand is not there yet. There is a disconnect. Customers say they want luxury goods handmade in France, but they are not willing to wait when a product becomes unavailable. This might work for a Hermès Birkin bag, but the flood of customers in luxury boutiques around the world want instant gratification. And brands are not willing to give up sales to a competitor that produces larger volumes using an industrial process. Customers say they want environmentally friendly leathers, but they also want to choose from a selection of colors beyond those that nontoxic processes can provide. And there are plenty of competitors willing to fill that demand. The competitive pressure on luxury brand managers is a barrier to their expressed desire to provide responsible leadership. In *The Good Struggle:*

Responsible Leadership in an Unforgiving World, Harvard Business School Professor Joseph Badaracco asks:

> What is responsible leadership when leaders confront so much uncertainty, when their jobs and their organizations seem temporary and fragile, when performance pressures focus everyone on short-term metrics, and when leaders don't have enough control of people and activities to deliver on longer-term commitments?[2]

Since the 1850s, society has been in the single-minded pursuit of economic growth. Building wealth has been the sole focus of economic policy and personal behavior as far back as anybody alive today can remember. It has been regarded as an objective good. Indeed, in the West during the Cold War years, growth was seen as a moral imperative, to prove capitalism's superiority over communism. With the fall of communism and the increase in globalization, that philosophy spread eastward and now dominates the globe. Even as Western cultures start to voice misgivings based on the social and environmental consequences of all this growth, an ostensibly communist China has embraced an aggressive business culture that would seem familiar to Westerners from two or three decades ago. But the West's misgivings are relatively new. Until recently, we paid little attention to the downsides of "anything goes" capitalism.

The reason for this is a business culture haunted by the ghost of economist Milton Friedman, who taught that the social responsibility of business is to make a profit.[3] Profit, wealth, and material comfort then become the proxy for the progress of civilization. This thinking underpins supply-side economic theory: economic growth based on cranking up production rather than meeting demand. Supply-side economics (make, market, and sell) shifted the focus of business from manufacturing a product in response to existing demand, to manufacturing demand that will absorb a product. It was reinforced by deregulation, financialization, and "trickle-down" economics, philosophies associated particularly with the 1980s and the pro-business attitudes of President Reagan in the US and Prime Minister Thatcher in the UK. Trickle-down economics argues that economic progress driven by the investment and expenditure of business and the upper classes keeps the whole of society employed, consuming, and prospering. It is an approach that fits neatly with the innate desire of humans to experience prosperity and improve their lot in life. Financial markets were deregulated, taxes on the wealthy lowered. And the investment, production, and marketing machines kicked into high gear.

The consequences of this have been manifold. It convinced a lot of people that they would be happier with more and better stuff. It created an acceleration of the consumption and competitive cycle, enabled by concurrent advances in technology. The pressures of speed and competition spurred people to prioritize work over personal life, to earn more, to move up the economic ladder, and to buy things that would move them up the social ladder. As a result, it has created a race to consume. Spend a Saturday afternoon at any shopping mall or high street and you will see shoppers buying reflexively, automatically, driven by what they are told to desire by marketers and by comparing their possessions with those of their peers. People feel compelled to buy, either so as not to feel "less than," or to feel "more like." The pre-assembled messages of brands have replaced values as a point of affiliation. Shopping is the new religion. The act of buying, simple possession, has taken on its own value, detached from the actual value of the product.

This same period and these same influences saw luxury brands transformed from independent, family or artisanal ownership to subsidiaries of large, professionally run conglomerates and financial holding companies. Along with the rest of business, they benefited from growth and globalization. This growth took them beyond their traditional customer base of society's elite and pushed luxury brands to reach towards the upper-middle and middle classes with brand extensions and products designed for entry level. Remember, only a generation ago, the vast majority of consumers could appreciate the prestige of a luxury brand, but they did not necessarily aspire to ownership. If they achieved it, that was an accomplishment. But nonachievement was not a failure because consumption had not yet become synonymous with fulfillment, and luxury had not yet become synonymous with self-worth. Now, accustomed to highly paced growth and under pressure to keep delivering products to consumers and returns to investors at the same rate, luxury brands, like consumers themselves, are trapped into staking their self-worth on economic growth. Of course they are, for luxury brands are ultimately composed of people who are bound to share the same habits as society at large.

The hidden costs of growth

Hannah Arendt, philosopher and political scientist, wrote: "Economic growth may one day turn out to be a curse rather than a good, and under no conditions can it either lead into freedom or constitute a proof for its existence."[4] While liberal economic policies since the 1980s have unleashed a wave of material gains, they have not actually brought the widespread egalitarian society for which prosperity was intended as a proxy. They may, in fact, have had the opposite effect. Even in rich countries, people are living less comfortably. After 30 years of Reaganomics, with mortgaged homes now filled with possessions and days spent working longer and harder to afford it all, it turns out that people are no wealthier, no happier, and the economic benefits, if anything, flood up rather than trickling down.

The oversized role of the financial sector in the global economy is one cause. By 2011, even after the damage caused by the financial crisis, the financial sector accounted for well over eight percent of US GDP.[5] While this sounds small, it is over four times its size in the 1950s, and compare it to the five percent of GDP attributed to the entire US automotive sector. Our processes and our attitudes towards the wellbeing of people have been geared to support the pursuit of money. More or less money is the binary framework for any institutional decision. Money, which was invented by people to serve their needs, facilitate transactions, and store value, has gone from servant to master. The consequences of this financialization are far-reaching and unpredictable.

One of the reasons that the US economy imploded was the rise of household debt. Home loans were a major part of this, but the overall debt was amplified by consumer credit that went to pay for electronic goods, cars, clothes, and holidays. Yet, as we spend, we do not seem to reap the benefits of the economic activity we are creating. While the trappings of wealth trickle down, more and more it seems that the actual wealth trickles up. The companies that make all the things we buy, and their owners, are the main beneficiaries. The cream of profits rises to the top, but then does not circle around again. While companies are sitting on mountains of cash, having returned to profitability in the recovery from the crisis, and investors have reaped the benefits of stock markets exceeding their pre-crisis highs, economic growth is still insecure and unemployment has remained stubbornly high. Even optimists predict a long, slow slog of a recovery until employment and consumer spending improve.

Luxury's broad customer base of middle- and upper-middle-class consumers is now eroding. Economic inequality has risen across developed countries. In fact, the growth of the past 30 years has masked the stagnation of middle-class wages and the decline of their living standards relative to the top. According to the Organisation for Economic Co-operation and Development

(OECD), which advises governments on how to improve the lives of their citizens: "Earners in the top 10% have been leaving the middle earners behind more rapidly than the lowest earners have been drifting away from the middle."[6] In 2013, the US's Urban Institute found that today's 20- to 40-year-olds will likely be the first generation in history less well off than the previous generation.[7] Barring inheritance, for many, their parents' lifestyles – their homes, financial security, and other comforts – the lifestyles these same people grew up with as children, now seem tantalizingly out of reach. Many of our parents and most of our grandparents managed to live quite well on a single income, within an eight-hour workday. They did so partly thanks to government subsidies for education and housing aimed to help the world recover from war and the Great Depression. But we have come to take their level of prosperity for granted. Today's middle-class parents both work, connected via laptops and smartphones into the night and on weekends, in order to match the standard of living of the previous generation.

These developments do not bode well for the future of luxury's growth. Luxury brands' dependence on middle-class customers exposes them to economic uncertainty in a way similar to other consumer goods. Luxury brands avoided the worst of the 2008–10 crisis only because of its uneven nature. The slowdown in the US and Europe shifted economic activity to new, emerging markets. In developed countries, governments responded to the crisis by pumping billions of dollars in bailout money into the banking system, which recovered quickly and was positioned to benefit disproportionately from the eventual recovery. High executive pay and multimillion-dollar bonuses continued to flow. But macroeconomic recovery from the crisis is slow and long, putting pressure on all society. While the rich may have gotten richer, the middle professional class on which luxury relies for sales volume is being squeezed by stagnating pay, higher taxes, continuing job insecurity, and uncertainty about the future. Hot emerging economies are cooling as well, removing the crutch that luxury brands used for their expansion through the depths of the crisis. With growth in developed countries insufficient to pick up the slack, luxury brands can expect a drawn-out period of slowing growth, if not outright contraction. Luxury companies are responding by trying to rekindle demand through new product and retail tactics, or by looking where they can tap new pockets of demand for existing approaches. They are slower to realize the tidal movements that are affecting the entire market and will do so over the long term.

It is not that luxury consumers will abandon luxury; they have become accustomed to luxury and will keep coming back. But they will look at luxury differently. As pressures and insecurities continue, they will approach luxury in a more disciplined, measured, discriminatory way, looking for forms of luxury that do not feel wasteful. This is much more profound than the trends that luxury brands have identified of luxury becoming more experiential and personal. Luxury has always been experiential and personal. This has to do with an entire shifting lifestyle on the part of the consumer, seeking to reconcile their work, their relationships and consumption into a single meaningful existence. Talk to the ideal customer for luxury brands – urban, well travelled, cultured, and entrepreneurial – and you hear similar themes emerge regardless of whether they are in Paris, New York, São Paulo, or Hong Kong: they still have a desire for luxury products but are increasingly unimpressed with the familiar offer and skeptical of the marketing spin. In the search for rarity, they are turning their backs on brands that are too omnipresent. Further, they talk about wanting to simplify their lives, with a focus on having fewer but better possessions and selectively curate the best, most interesting, most innovative products. They are looking for meaning in their purchases by choosing brands that are the best for the product rather than the most glamorous. Like buying a luxury watch from a renowned watchmaker rather than an of-the-moment fashion brand. They want to trust the brands they buy to contribute to their holistic aims.

The breakdown of trust

There is another, more complex aspect to trust in the context of luxury. This has to do with the breakdown of trust in society as a whole, affecting trust in institutions and, by extension, trust of leaders and elites. Starting in 2008, as cash flow dried up, business activity slowed, workers were laid off, and government programs were cut, faith was lost in the system and its leaders. The financial crisis became an economic crisis, which became a social crisis, which became a crisis of confidence. It is now a crisis of leadership. Anthony Gooch of the OECD dubbed it the "crisis domino effect." The crisis caused a breakdown of the social contract, in which the public accepts the privileges of its leaders so long as they are seen as stewards of security and wellbeing. When the crisis threw the latter into question, the public lost faith in government, which was seen as too influenced by business interests. As a result, the economic establishment came under suspicion, as did the wealthy, global plutocracy that is seen as running it. Trust in large companies and other institutions, and in their leadership, is at an all-time low. A 2011 study by global PR firm Burson-Marsteller found that trust had fallen across the board as a result of the crisis, when it came to international companies, corporate executives, international organizations, and especially governments.[8] By 2013, public trust in the governments of OECD countries, for 60 years the role models for sound economic development, stood at around 40 percent.[9]

The crisis highlighted irresponsible, even illegal practices among some of our most trusted institutions. The crisis wiped out people's savings, jobs, and homes across the economy, but it barely touched the financial sector that had caused it. Banks continued and continue to turn a profit and rationalize the payment of fortunes in bonuses to their employees, even as they survived thanks to bailouts from the public coffers. Revered banks like Lehman Brothers and Bear Sterns collapsed through irresponsible risk taking. Governments stepped in to save others, protecting private money with the public's money. As a result, the major banks have all come under increasing and increasingly antagonistic public, media, and government scrutiny of their actions leading up to, during, and after the crisis. They are incurring stiffer regulations with regard to their reserve requirements and compensation. In 2014, Goldman Sachs, Morgan Stanley, JP Morgan, Citigroup, Bank of America, and Wells Fargo all reported earnings eroded by fines and legal fees.

The case for how once dependable brands abused their clients' (and the public) money is by now well established. This is to say nothing of how they abused their clients' trust. When Greg Smith, a senior Goldman Sachs executive, resigned in 2012, he sent a scathing editorial to *The New York Times* denouncing the company's "toxic and destructive" environment.[10] Bankers dismissed their clients as "muppets" and put the financial interests of the bank ahead of those whose money had been entrusted to it. Smith's exposé triggered no introspection on the part of the bank's leadership. Naturally, Lloyd Blankfein, Goldman Sachs' CEO, replied with the predictable rejoinder that Smith's accusations did not reflect the firm's values.[11] But this was the same company that had bet against securities on their own account while aggressively marketing them to their clients. Perhaps unsurprising from a CEO who had joked in the darkest depths of the crisis that he was "doing God's work."[12]

While luxury brands hardly caused the chain of events that led to the breakdown in trust, they are vulnerable to contagion from its effects. There is a two-pronged effect. First, as the lack of trust in institutions creates generalized fear and anxiety, people become more skeptical of brands deemed too institutional and with a too obviously manufactured image, favoring instead those with which they can establish a more authentic, personal relationship. This is compounded by the second prong, which is the association of luxury with those who have abused their positions of power. Sociologist Philip Slater described wealth addiction in 1980.[13] More than 30 years later, Sam Polk, a former hedge fund trader, now founder of the nonprofit Groceryships, described this phenomenon from personal experience:

> Wealth addicts are responsible for the vast and toxic disparity between the rich and the poor and the annihilation of the middle class ... Only a wealth addict would earn hundreds of millions as a hedge-fund manager, and then lobby to maintain a tax loophole that gave him a lower tax rate than his secretary.[14]

When perceptions of leaders become tarnished, luxury brands become symbols of their wealth addiction and greed. They get caught up in the class struggle.

The social schism has made its way into the popular culture, which now increasingly derides wealth rather than celebrating it. Take, for example, 2011's futuristic film *In Time*, or 2010's *The Company Men*. In both films, a rarefied circle remains immune and indifferent to the travails of commoners. In Andrew Niccol's *In Time*, poverty is an acutely existential concern, as money has been replaced by time. When you run out of it, you die on the spot. The average person hopes to hold on to 24 hours in a day, so that they can live long enough to be paid again, while an immortal elite keeps raising prices to keep the masses indentured. Without going to the extremes of science fiction, John Wells' *The Company Men* takes place in the tangible reality of post-crisis, suburban America. While company layoffs cut ever closer to the executive inner circle, the boss builds himself a lavish new office. One executive's wife listens tetchily to her husband's qualms before asking if she can borrow the corporate jet for a weekend shopping spree. In 2013, Martin Scorsese's *The Wolf of Wall Street* stirred tremendous debate about whether the film's portrayal of a real-life financial villain celebrates his bad behavior or holds up an example of society's appetite for wealth run amok to the point of depravity.

Revolutionary thinking

The debate about class and income inequality, the loss of faith in the establishment, the emergence of new ideas about consumption and the economy are all echoes of the agitated movements of 100 years ago. The Industrial Revolution had caused similar concerns when production technology upended established social orders by creating new sources of wealth and thus new power structures and relationships in society. So technological revolution is a precursor of social revolution, or rather social evolution. Similarly, today's debates are emerging from the opportunities and challenges that have been created by IT. The crisis of 2008 was a choke point. In converging technological change, globalization, a century of growing consumerism and consequent debates about values, sustainability, business ethics, and corporate responsibility, the crisis was the world gagging on its own abundance.

Technology, for all the possibility it provides – the creative capabilities, the access to information, the channels for interconnection – also increases speed and interdependence. It multiplies complicating factors and reduces our response times. The combination increases risk exponentially. Systems become too big and tangled for people to grapple with. Problems become more difficult to predict, spot, and solve. As a result, we have amplified our footprint and the impacts of our behavior to where they cause conflict and breakdowns. Speed and interdependence are cited among the causes of the 2008 crisis, in which innovative new financial instruments were supposed to spread risk and adapt it to the tolerance of various investor groups. Instead, they ended up creating complicated packages of securities that even professionals found difficult to understand and that concealed the weakness of the assets they included, notably the infamous subprime mortgages. This was exacerbated by the interconnection of financial markets around the world and their increasing reliance on IT in their processes. Trading decisions now use computer-generated algorithms to assess risks, returns, and timing. Human instinct, doubt, and common sense get removed from the equation. High-frequency trading is the ultimate example, where large blocks of corporate shares, currencies, derivatives, and other products are bought and resold in the blink of an eye. In these transactions, the advantage goes to the trader with the fastest software and computers rather than the one with the keenest insight and analysis of the products they trade. By some estimates, high-frequency trading has reduced the average length of share ownership in companies from a matter of years to a matter of seconds. Largely unregulated, in 2009 it accounted for almost three-fourths of financial market transactions and still accounts for about half of them today.

The result is a fundamental shift in the relationship between owners and their assets, shareholders and their companies. Owner interest in a company's long-term prospects is replaced by speculation on the short-term movement of its shares. Indeed, there is an incentive to manipulate markets so that fast-paced bets can arbitrage between the misalignments. In this environment, it is difficult if not impossible to invest the time and thought necessary for stable and sustainable returns. Even a company that wants to do so is vulnerable to the quick to and fro of speculation. It creates an entire culture of ever shorter term thinking and reactivity.

But technology is neutral, a tool. It only does what we tell it to, so the consequences of technology can respond to how we use it. Part of the complexity we describe is a result of IT giving us the means to equip ourselves with information, to connect communities of like-minded people and create movements, to challenge conventional notions and established institutions. The Arab Spring is an example of the empowering aspects of IT, particularly social media. With it, an otherwise fragmented public was able to use its broadly shared feeling of dissatisfaction to coalesce and mobilize against a well-organized body. For institutions, social media is certainly a dynamic and convivial channel for building more personal relations with a brand's customers and broader fanbase. But the real power of the technology embodied by our cozy Facebook pages has much bigger and more volatile implications. The massive online disclosures of classified government documents by Edward Snowden, a former CIA employee, and Chelsea (formerly Bradley) Manning, a US Army soldier, show how the challenge can come from within an organization, even in the form of a single, junior member. Technology renders organizations transparent. If a luxury brand's reputation is its greatest asset, the radical transparency brought on by technology presents either a huge risk or a fantastic opportunity, depending on how honest – with itself – a company is prepared to be. This is revolutionary thinking that emerges from technological revolution.

Contrary to popular belief, revolutions do not come from the abject bottom. The crowds of the Arab Spring, the Occupy Movement, the Greek riots and Los Indignados gathering in the streets of, for example, Cairo, New York, London, Athens, and Madrid were not led by the starving poor. The lowest classes are often too disenfranchised and disempowered to even be able to act on their own behalf. Instead, revolutions come from the middle and the intelligentsia, from those with a close enough view of the top to aspire to its ranks, but who become overwhelmed by the injustice and frustration of exclusion. The mass of the bottom provides the muscle, but it is the middle, professional and intellectual classes that shape and organize a movement, and give direction to its seething anger. They have the "luxury" of education and the security to pursue higher level needs that enable them to focus on ideals, not just on survival. This middle is also precisely the market that luxury brands have been wooing in their pursuit of growth.

The revolution brewing now is not about storming palaces and chopping off heads. Cairo, Tunis, and Tripoli were flashpoints in response to specific situations only marginally linked to the global malaise. The wider revolution is much more tempered and introspective, aimed at reforming rather than removing institutions, based on a rethinking of values and priorities that people had voluntarily adhered to until now, but which are evolving with life experience. We are not witnessing emerging values in conflict with established beliefs. Rather we are seeing people integrate new thinking with established practice.

Disillusioned by the false promise of growth and prosperity, people are focusing more on their own definition of success. They are aiming for satisfaction and fulfillment rather than acclaim. In 2013, Erin Callan, the former CFO of Lehman Brothers, wrote in an editorial titled "Is there life after work" about how much her singular career drive cost her on a personal level.[15] She wrote: "The fact that I call it 'the rest of my life' gives you an indication of where work stood in the pecking order." Obsessive discipline had gotten her to the top, but she laments the personal sacrifices: her failed first marriage, not having a child. It is a very public echo of others whose lives were turned upside-down by the financial crisis, but who found greater self-knowledge, empowerment, and fulfillment as a result. These people took the crisis as an opportunity to start their own businesses or move to smaller communities where the real cost of living – the pace of life and the shape of ambitions – do not require so much sacrifice.

This approach extends to a fundamental change in consumer habits and more sophisticated ideas about luxury. The overabundance we enjoyed up until now clashes with our increased awareness of the resources that go into it and the waste that results, including our own resources: the time spent working to earn the money spent buying, as well as natural resources: the trees that are used to make packaging, the energy that is used for production and transport. What happens to all the stuff once we are done with it? The fashion cycle pushes us to buy and dispose every season. Even durable goods, such as appliances and electronics, now have obsolescence built in. Last year's model does not work with this year's software. The worn-out part makes the whole gadget cheaper to replace than to repair. It all accumulates around us, in our homes, our garbage dumps, our oceans, and gets ever more difficult to ignore. The emphasis shifts to consuming more responsibly and living more sustainably, not just in terms of the planet, but in terms of oneself.

These tastes are opening new channels, like the Slow Movement, which seek to reconnect production and consumption with natural processes and rhythms, holding at bay pressures of ever increasing speed and scale. The Slow Movement began as Slow Food in 1986 in Italy, where the opening of a McDonald's at the Spanish Steps in Rome prompted national food producers to resist the homogenization of food production and the encroachment of industrialization on gastronomy. Slow Food has since become a worldwide phenomenon, with a network in 150 countries that organizes events promoting local farmers, flavors, and artisans. Slow has also spread into other fields. The Slow Movement manifesto was signed in Paris in 1989, and has spawned branches focused on Slow Fashion, Slow Finance, Slow Urbanism, Cittaslow, and others. In France, Slow Made is building a new economic model that eschews high quantity and low cost in favor of quality design, materials and manufacturing, a relationship between producer and consumer, a respect for time and longevity, and prices that reflect the value of these resources. With this sensibility, Slow is a close cousin of luxury. According to Marc Bayard, counselor for cultural and scientific development at France's Mobilier National and a founder of Slow Made, "the common point between Slow and luxury is their respect for materials and processes with inherent rarity," adding that luxury has the capacity to inspire the consumer to new practices. By rediscovering and applying the lessons that industrialized luxury prefers to forget, Slow could very well become the new fount of luxury.

In a similar vein, 1.618 Paris, an organization dedicated to promoting sustainable development in the luxury sector, showcase brands demonstrating a new vision of luxury, which integrates creativity, quality and emotion with sustainable development. 1.618 Paris work closely with an independent committee of experts in environmental and social responsibility, design, sociology, and economics who assess the characteristics of each brand according to these criteria. The brands represent a range of products, from hotels to surfboards and startups to globally recognized brands such as BMW's i series and Six Senses hotels, resorts and spas. According to Barbara Coignet, founder of 1.618 Paris: "luxury and sustainable development are not only compatible by nature but also co-dependent." According to 1.618 Paris, real luxury is, by definition, durable and serves as a role model for sustainability through its propensity to create value, support local economies, and protect resources. Meanwhile, sustainable development needs luxury to redefine the dreams of the 21st century and benefits from luxury's visibility to inspire new behaviors, allowing consumers to participate in building a better world.

There are several examples. Norlha opened a workshop in the impoverished nomadic lands of the Tibetan plateau, and work with local tribes to produce yak wool textiles. They weave it themselves rather than selling the raw material at low cost, and give it additional value by transforming it into luxury goods with stronger commercial potential. As part of the brand's work, it has taught its workers to read and count, empowering them with skills to participate in the broader economy, while simultaneously instilling pride in their traditional culture and an incentive to maintain it. On the opposite end of the spectrum, Cottin, based in Paris, manufacture computers housed in artisanal cases made with fine woods, leathers, marquetry, and jewelry. The focus is on the entire product life cycle, from a short, locally based supply chain, to improved repairability and sustainability.

Soneva Resorts, a hotel brand with nightly rates reaching into the thousands of dollars at properties in Thailand and the Maldives, follow the philosophical acronym of SLOW LIFE (sustainable, local, organic, wellness, learning, inspiring, fun, experiences).[16] This marries the Slow approach with other notions such as barefoot luxury and sustainable luxury. Everything still has to be superlative, but it turns traditional notions of luxury on its head. Luxury is no longer a thousand-dollar shoe. Rather, it is no shoe at all. And they go further still by establishing a positive relationship with the local community, minimizing or even enhancing their environmental impact.

What ties all these examples together is their combination of hedonistic pleasure with a feeling of doing good somewhere in the world. The external validation that was once enjoyed when carrying a particular brand is being replaced by the first-hand rewards that come from a sense of authenticity, responsibility, and connection. For habitual trendsetters, if this means seeking out little known, niche brands to be the first on the block with a new product, all the better. In this context, knowledge rather than price becomes the qualifier for exclusivity. And rarity is based on the actual scarcity of the product and skill, rather than on holding back supply to create a frenzy of desire. Conspicuous consumption slowly loses out to intelligent consumption. There will always be both kinds of customers. The question for luxury brands is whether they want to represent excess or intellect.

Luxury's opportunity for leadership

Leaders must look beyond the self-justifying worldview of their own experience. Leaders need to be able to connect with the needs, motivations, and emotions of those they seek to inspire to follow them. This is the leadership mandate for luxury brands.

According to a 2012 study by global PR firm Edelman: "The power of Purpose is driving consumer preference and loyalty in a world where trust in corporations is low and differentiation between brands is negligible." People are drawn to luxury because it promises them a better future: fully 87 percent of consumers believe that business should equally balance social and business interests.[17] Viewed this way, luxury brands' distinction is about more than their aesthetic, it is about improving the lives of the people connected to the brand. Consumers, especially luxury consumers, already have products in abundance. What they really want are meaning and solutions, if not through the product itself, then at least through the process by which the product comes into being.

Luxury brands must position themselves as a bulwark against the race to the bottom. They need to use their strengths – their cultural influence, their embodiment of progress, their ability to create desire – to build a new kind of business approach. They must provide a desirable alternative to consumers already looking to escape the vicious cycle of blind consumption and open the eyes of others to the freedom that can be had from buying judiciously and investing in quality. Upending luxury's current practices, returning to time-tested ideals of the past, luxury must link elite status with a kind of social stewardship.

One of the main brakes on socially valuable business is that consumers are not willing to compromise on quality or pay more. The critical mass for the necessary economies of scale takes time to develop. But here, luxury has an advantage: its ultimate concern is quality and its consumers' price elasticity puts critical mass within reach at lower levels of quantity. Further, the aspirational attributes of luxury brands give them the power to drive societal values and behaviors; to lead by example. This means going beyond "social add-ons" to a systemic transformation. This means going beyond scrambling to do good in PR-friendly areas to making a long-term commitment in only those areas where the brand has meaning and can make a significant impact. This means creating programs with depth, which engage internal stakeholders, consumers, and external partners in achieving the necessary scale. It means drawing on the values of the brand to communicate a holistic value proposition that unites the business with the community it inhabits and with the individuals that comprise both.

This leadership position is wide open.

Notes

1   Kirkland, R. (2013) "Leading in the 21st century: An interview with Société Générale's Frédéric Oudéa." *McKinsey Quarterly*, November.

2   Badaracco, J. Jr. (2013) *The Good Struggle: Responsible Leadership in an Unforgiving World*, p. 3. Harvard Business School Press.

3   Friedman, M. (1970) "The social responsibility of business is to increase its profits." *The New York Times Magazine*, September 13.

4   Arendt, H. (1990) *On Revolution*. Penguin.

5   Lahart, J. (2011) "Number of the week." *The Wall Street Journal*, December 10. Quoting data from the U.S. Department of Commerce.

6   OECD (2011) *Divided We Stand: Why Inequality Keeps Rising.* OECD.

7   Steuerle, E. (2013) "Lost generations?: Wealth building among young Americans." Urban Institute Working Papers, March.

8   *Trust and Purpose Survey 2011.* Burson-Marsteller and Penn Schoen Berland.

9   OECD (2013) *Government at a Glance 2013.* OECD.

10 Smith, G. (2012) "Why I am leaving Goldman Sachs." *The New York Times*, March 14.

11 WSJ Staff (2012) "Goldman memo: We were disappointed to read assertions." *The Wall Street Journal. Deal Journal* blog, March 14.

12 Dealbook (2009) "Blankfein says he's just doing 'God's Work'." *The New York Times*, November 9.

13 Slater, P. (1980) *Wealth Addiction.* E.P. Dutton.

14 Polk, S. (2014) "For the love of money." *The New York Times*, January 18.

15 Callan, E. (2013) "Is there life after work." *The New York Times*, March 9.

16 www.soneva.com.

17 Edelman (2012) *Goodpurpose 2012: Global Consumer Survey.*

4

Luxury and the search for meaning

- Definitions of value are becoming more complex as the world shifts from an institutional focus to an individual focus and from an economy of things to an economy of ideas.

- Brands must evolve from being businesses to being citizens.

- New ways of working go beyond following instructions to the kind of open-ended thinking necessary for leadership and creating art.

Our premise in this book is that luxury brands have an innate leadership capacity. They can build business models that are in tune with the evolving expectations of society and serve as role models for individuals and other companies. Further, by working like artists, beyond the constraints imposed by markets, luxury brands can affirm the very essence of what qualifies them as luxury: the ability to present a point of view that shapes how people think and what they desire. To do so, however, they must shed certain entrenched and outdated assumptions about what people expect of luxury. Class, status, and aspiration are becoming ever more ad hoc notions, anchored more in an individual's psyche and personal values than in the dictates of a social hierarchy. So, luxury firms must think laterally about the value they offer, how that value is encapsulated and communicated through their brands, and how they go about building it through their work.

Value was once contained in the practical function of a product. Then, in the mid-20th century, companies learned to manufacture demand by playing on consumers' emotions. Rather than being set by the simple market forces of supply and demand, value started being determined by a wider group of stakeholders. Suddenly, the transaction dialogue became a peanut gallery of the opinions of friends, family, neighbors, colleagues, and so on. This means that if value used be a reflection of the price the consumer would accept for a given product, today value is an infinitely more complicated calculation, balancing features and perceptions, real and imagined benefits, and financial and psychological costs. What was once a label, a maker's mark, which then evolved into a point of lifestyle affiliation, is now a signifier of a philosophy, a culture, and a set of values that the consumer can support, ignore, or disparage.

If, in the past, the brand belonged to the artisan, founder, or manufacturer, it is quickly becoming community property. Tomorrow, the brand will be an even more nuanced corporate identity, based on the company's role in an interdependent world. It will encompass aspects of being a manufacturer, an employer, and a neighbor – a complete member of society. And, as society's most visible citizens, brands are expected to show leadership. This is where luxury brands in particular can excel. Figure 4.1 shows this evolution of value, brands and the nature of work from being imposed by the market to being rooted in art and leadership.

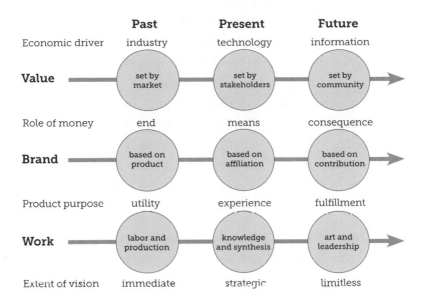

FIGURE 4.1 The evolution of value, brands and work

The abstraction and fragmentation of value

Human existence has been characterized by a single theme since the beginning of civilization: the search for knowledge and meaning. This is true of individuals and society as a whole. The 4th-century Greek philosopher Plato identified the meaning of life as attaining the highest form of knowledge, from which all things derive utility and value. Aristotle, his student, evolved this thinking further to conclude that ethical knowledge is general knowledge, giving people the ability to think and act virtuously. This evolution had parallels in cultures and religions beyond the Western tradition, being at the heart of Hinduism and Buddhism. In the 17th century, René Descartes coined the phrase "cogito ergo sum" – I think therefore I am. His peers, Enlightenment philosophers, applied previous ideas of knowledge and virtue to the relationship between individuals, and between an individual and society at large, leading to civic notions of freedom, equality, rights, and citizenship. Ultimately, with the rise of science over faith in contributing to our knowledge, these streams of thought were integrated into the study of human psychology and neurology in an effort to trace thousands of years of philosophy to its biological origins. That is not to ignore its application in everyday life. Even Adam Smith, the 18th-century author of *The Wealth of Nations* and founding father of economics as a profession, was not an economist but a moral philosopher. He was not so much interested in money as in the efficient and ethical distribution of resources throughout society.

The pursuit of meaning and knowledge generated two, more tangible phenomena that have direct implications for brands: the abstraction of value and the fragmentation of society, which together diminish the authority of institutions.

Value was originally based on growth because resources were physical. To create value, a society had to conquer new territories. Richness came from empire building, allowing countries to access and control larger quantities of land and people to extract raw materials, minerals, crops, labor, skills, taxes, and so on. Individual success was also measured in the accumulation of wealth, leading to influence and power over others. Businesses were the machinery of empire building in the colonial era. They followed in the steps of explorers, missionaries, and ideological pioneers to establish commercial control of new territories and administer the transfer of wealth back to the home country. Modern companies are the heirs of this legacy, which explains the continuity of this belief system in business right through industrialization and into the modern era. Business and, by extension, economic processes and governments are still centered on growth as a means of security, stability, and status. This translates to the individual propensity to measure success according to wealth.

But, as we established earlier, people are shifting their focus away from material prosperity to a broader vision of quality of life, which balances wealth with ideals of health, happiness, meaning, and fulfillment. At the broadest level, we see how this awakening is changing the way government thinks. New measures are challenging the primacy of GDP for determining the prosperity of countries. The Kingdom of Bhutan got the ball rolling in the early 1970s with a Gross National Happiness indicator to accompany its economic progress measures. Long considered a curiosity among economists and social scientists, it began to serve as a model for others as the idea of sustainable development gained traction through the 1980s and 90s. The United Nations (UN) launched the Human Development Index in 1990, measuring national incomes alongside life expectancy and education. After the 2008 recession caused many to question the organization of economic systems and the imperative of growth, other measures entered the game of defining more subjective measures of progress. State statistical agencies in Australia, Canada, China, France, and the UK subsequently began to ask their citizens how they were doing emotionally, not just materially. The constitutions of Ecuador and Bolivia identify quality of life as the goal of sustainable development. The OECD launched their Better Life Index in 2011, measuring 36 countries' performance according to 11 indicators, including income as well as areas such as civic engagement, personal support networks, work–life balance, and self-reported life satisfaction.

The second phenomenon, driven by the pursuit of wellbeing and fulfillment, is the steady drift of civilization from placing value on institutions to placing value on individuals. It is the common thread that binds the emancipation of slaves and serfs, the recognition of fundamental human rights, the rise of republics, universal suffrage, civil rights, the fall of communism, the waning influence of organized religion, right through to the rise of social media. Historically, people were dependent on institutional benefactors for their survival, security, and wellbeing. Way back, this role was fulfilled by tribal structures, which eventually evolved into feudal, martial, and monarchic systems with close ties to religious establishments. While even those autocratic systems governed only with the consent of the governed, the disparity in the information, influence, and authority allotted between rulers and their subjects was such that the social contract remained relatively stable. With industrialization, civilian government and business assumed the bulk of political and economic power. This was the first, great worldwide social upheaval. With varied levels of efficiency and fairness, these new structures ensured that resources were distributed throughout society well enough to maintain order. Through them, a new social contract was born: no longer rigid and hereditary but more flexible, juridical, and mercantile, into which one entered voluntarily and within which one could navigate and negotiate one's lot.

Now, these too are changing. Developments in IT during the past decade have allowed this fragmentation from institutions to individuals to truly take hold. Since 2000, thanks to the rapid growth of the Internet, its convergence with mobile technology, and the advent of social media, societal structures are breaking down and the established rules of the game are changing. Technology gives us access and the ability to exchange a vast amount of information, which provides a powerful platform for expression, creativity, and innovation. Individual voices now have many more outlets than institutional voices did just a few decades ago. This has changed the power dynamic. It has broken the control of large, established entities over their territory and lowered barriers to entry for even the smallest competitors for political influence and market share. For example, after less than a decade in existence, *The Huffington Post*, a "blog of blogs," now stands shoulder to shoulder as a media platform and influencer with venerated, century-old titles like *The New York Times* and *Le Monde*, having won a Pulitzer Prize and launched international editions in seven languages.

What we are experiencing now is a fragmentation of traditional structures, which will eventually lead to new social, economic, and political systems. As technology increases transparency, order will come less from structural skeletons, but rather – like the stones in an arch – from the pressures we exert on one another.

As a result of these two phenomena, people are free to design and pursue work they love in the knowledge that passion is a more reliable path to fulfillment than the material success from a series of promotions. Even baby boomers, who had grown prosperous by following well worn career paths, are not indifferent to new ways of thinking about a more balanced way of living and working. In a networked world, all value has a chance of finding its market rather than having to conform to a role predefined by an institution. Generations X and Y grew up with the opportunities fostered by mass media and the Internet, and no longer feel obliged to aim for the security that a corporate career path provides. To these generations, work looks more like a productive form of play rather than toil. If the baby boomers are thinking about work–life balance, the younger generations are focused on work–life blending, where both form a single, pleasurable existence. If earlier societies and markets depended on the efficient organization and distribution of labor, today people can reorganize themselves into like-minded communities and markets that are independent of geographic proximity and even personal contact. People no longer have to live in big cities and commercial capitals in order to connect to markets and prosper. The opportunities provided by technology offer liberating alternatives with greater personal and professional autonomy. Generation Z, now in elementary school, accustomed from birth to having a world of knowledge and possibilities at their disposal, will be even more inclined in this direction.

Value is no longer defined in monetary terms. It is now qualitative, individual, even fluid.

How brands create meaning

The importance of this evolution for brands cannot be overestimated. On the one hand, companies are being challenged to relate to individuals – internal and external stakeholders alike – in a way that responds to their search for wellbeing, meaning, and fulfillment. On the other hand, brands have lost the lock on authority and the ability to control definitive messages.

It is forcing businesses to think long term and holistically about their activities and integrate more sustainable and socially responsible practices that respond to individuals' concerns. Brands are being asked to behave like fully fledged citizens of the community and not just businesses in a marketplace. What was once a civil society argument from NGOs and consumer protection movements for corporate ethics is now gaining traction within the business establishment. Originally arising from public pressure and social and consumer activism, responsible business is increasingly supported, even demanded, by employees and investors. Companies are realizing that to attract and retain the best talent, they have to offer more than rising career paths and comfortable wages and benefits. They also need to provide meaningful work that gives employees a sense of contributing to the bigger picture. Socially responsible investment funds, such as the Domini Social Equity Fund, the Appleseed Fund, and the Winslow Green Growth Fund, once fringe vehicles, are becoming more mainstream and garnering coverage from the financial media. So are stock market indices, such as the Advanced Sustainable Performance

Indices, FTSE4Good, and the Dow Jones Sustainability Indices, which help investors track companies' combined financial, environmental, and social performance.

Beyond that, companies must be sure that these practices are fully integrated into their corporate culture and ways of working, not just projected to enhance their brand image. With institutional trust at an all-time low, individuals are more likely to believe one another than any "official" positions coming from within the brand. The whole of a brand image used to be based on centrally controlled and crafted corporate messages. Through their corporate communications, advertising, and marketing machines they had influence over public opinion. Now, however, they compete with a mass of independent, unaccountable, and even anonymous voices – bloggers, social media followers, and others – who are forever scrutinizing brand messages, comparing them with company behavior, and broadcasting their experiences spontaneously and instantaneously to a vast audience. Any intern with an Instagram account and a viral capacity in the tens of thousands has the potential to torpedo a well-tended brand image. Controlling brand image today is a complicated affair, a 360-degree reality check; perilous if there is even a hint of inauthenticity.

Authenticity is therefore a key ingredient of meaning, the search for which is at the heart of the human condition. The luxury customer is even more sensitive to meaning because it is what explains the difference between the physical value of a luxury product and its price. The meaning of a luxury product to the customer is potentially limitless, which is what gives the customer enormous price elasticity and allows luxury brands to charge higher prices.

The uncompromising nature at the origin of luxury brands has allowed them to build the reputations they have today. Their pursuit of perfection was the characteristic that endeared them to their elite customers and, by extension and aspiration, to the larger public. The product gave meaning to the brand in those days. Hermès Sellier and Louis Vuitton Malletier, the complete, original names of two of today's most powerful luxury brands, speak to their very specific origins as saddlers and trunk makers. The brand was more of a maker's mark than the brands we know today. If a certain artisan was more sought after thanks to a royal warrant or by being fashionable among a style-setting elite, the benefits were more in the steady stream of commissions rather than the ability to charge a premium based solely on image. Advertising, to the extent that it existed, was focused on raising awareness and stirring desire for one's own product over a competitor's. It had not yet evolved to manufacturing a desire that did not already exist. Manufacturers competed on product attributes that were innate to the company and its way of working, not on abstract notions of meaning.

In the postwar period, with the expansion of mass media and the ripening of the advertising and marketing professions, brands developed broader lifestyle value propositions. The widening and diversification of product offerings mandated this change to give meaning to a more heterogeneous brand offering. It was a natural evolution, as houses worked to keep up with the times and integrate the visions of new ownership as they passed from one generation to the next, or took on new investors and creative directors. Coco Chanel, who started out making hats and grew into women's wear, took her vision of the modern, emancipated woman from clothes to fragrance in 1920, with the launch of Chanel No. 5. Louis Vuitton followed a natural progression from making trunks to smaller cases attuned to evolving travel and dress styles: air travel, shorter trips, less formal attire, and so on. Bags intended for everyday use eventually became the mainstay of the brand, which went even further in the 1990s, expanding into apparel, watches, even interior objects and books. Younger brands, such as Christian Dior, Yves Saint Laurent, and Ralph Lauren emerged directly with a varied product mix, or quickly leveraged their reputations in one field, such as fashion, to conquer others, such as fragrance and cosmetics. Versace, Armani, and Bulgari have stretched their brands as far as the hotel sector. In 2009, Hermès collaborated with Wally, an Italian shipbuilder, on a revolutionary design for a yacht. With products often developed under license agreements, the brand went from being a maker's mark to a kind of endorsement of the wares produced by others under its aegis. Rather than being defined by a product, the brand became a signifier of a lifestyle. The lifestyle projected by a brand gave it its meaning by representing not just the customer's possessions, but their values and affiliations.

Today, customers expect brands to provide meaning and social media provides possibilities for audience engagement. This pushes brands further still: many have developed content that takes brand communications from the traditional function of marketing to realms such as exposé and editorial. Whether it is a blog or Twitter feed disseminating a day in the life of a celebrity designer, or elaborate films made in collaboration with artists and directors, product brands are slowly turning into media platforms. As early as 2001, Bulgari commissioned acclaimed English author Fay Weldon to write *The Bulgari Connection*, a novel that integrated the brand into its storyline about British high society. This effort is almost quaint compared with more recent initiatives. LVMH's digital magazine, *Nowness*, describes itself as a "curated destination for the culturally curious, a point of reference for leaders in media and style, and a creative community committed to discovering, crafting and showcasing exceptional work, in collaboration with exceptional artists."[1] Its content is available in English, French, and Chinese. While LVMH brands do appear in its articles and videos, competing brands, such as Cartier, Gucci, and Chanel, also get an airing. Other topics carry no brand references whatsoever, focusing exclusively on dancers, musicians, novelists, other artists, and celebrities. Setting brands into a cultural context by creating a larger universe is the transformation of meaning from a product and lifestyle affiliation to an artistic and intellectual one.

Meaning is a combination of understanding the origins of something with its relevance to an individual in the present moment. For a brand that seeks to be timeless, as luxury brands do, relevance must also be projected into the future, so that the brand and the product can retain their value. This means taking a strong position for the brand today while grappling with the uncertainty innate to the evolution of society. It is impossible to predict future values and tastes. Here, intent matters in creating and maintaining value. Going back to the debates of ancient philosophers, who were preoccupied with the achievement and perpetuation of knowledge as the source of virtue and value, this means that meaning depends on the contribution of the brand to society – its purpose. So what contribution can a luxury brand make?

The work of art

The purpose of luxury is contained in its role as an applied art form. Indeed, we established in Chapter 1, given time, luxury goods become artworks by their preservation and transmission over generations until they are eventually displayed in museums. Art is no mere leisurely diversion. It helps us deal with uncertainty. Art serves an essential role in boosting the intellectual process by helping us grapple with abstraction, teaching us to analyze complex, even incomplete information, challenging established assumptions about the world.

A work of art is an invitation to dialogue. This is particularly true of modern art. Beginning with impressionism in the late 1800s, and moving through fauvism, cubism, dada, surrealism, and to even more radical forms we see today, art has become less about representing the existing world and more about expressing emotional and intellectual ideas. It became less about conforming to rules than about exploring new territories. The modern artist puts out work that is not meant to be definitive but open to the viewer's own perception, interpretation, adaptation, and appropriation. The art comes from the artist and it is created for the artist, as a form of self-actualization. But it is not about the artist. It is about the world.

With online, visual media making up a greater part of our information intake, the artistic abilities to both create and interpret are now crucial. In many instances, passive education via mass media consumption is displacing more traditional forms of learning. This gives art a direct and urgent role in helping people accurately understand the world. One study by Australian researchers looked into the use of the Internet by children to educate themselves about human sexuality. The study revealed that driven by natural curiosity, children explore online representations of sex at earlier ages than schools and parents had anticipated. But the very specific nature of the images they discover (we are talking about pornography here) leaves them vulnerable to developing skewed and unhealthy attitudes towards human sexuality – unless they have an underlying ability to contextualize the information. As the study explains: "To be unable to critique imagery is equivalent to being illiterate in the modern world."[2]

Alvin Toffler, the American futurist and expert in the communication revolution, puts it another way: "The illiterate of the 21st Century will not be those who cannot read and write, but those who cannot learn, unlearn and relearn." Here again, art is crucial because it is open-ended and ever evolving. If we are comfortable with art, we are comfortable with subjectivity and uncertainty. These are the two overwhelming characteristics of the increasingly abstract and fragmented society we describe. When information and power are completely democratized, when social structures are no longer anchored by institutions, but depend on a vast and complex web of individual interactions, we are stripped of the illusion of a reliable, predictable future. Rather than plodding a charted course, we must be able to adapt to ever evolving circumstances. To do that without getting lost, we must be able to envision what we are aiming for.

Luxury gives us this vision. Luxury's link to art is based on more than a shared affinity for beauty. It is based in their mutual ability to abstract the meaning of value. Take the example of Ai Weiwei's exhibition *Dropping the Urn*, where he transforms 5,000-year-old Chinese pottery by smashing it, dipping it in industrial paint, or applying commercial logos. Here, the link between luxury and art has three dimensions. One, the vessels, by dint of their age and anthropological value, are revered as art. To be able to possess one is a luxury. Two, their transformation (some would say their destruction)

> strips them of their aura of preciousness only to reapply it according to a different system of valuation ... The substitution of one kind of value for another occurs when he displays the transformed urns in a museum vitrine, reinstilling value but replacing historical significance with a newer cultural one.[3]

Finally, there is luxury in the artist's use of a rare and precious object towards his own ends. These three dimensions combine to create a comment on the destruction of ancient culture by modernity and call our attention in a dramatic way to what we choose to value. Is it the ancient object or the artistic expression? Which vase would you pay more for as a collector? In both its form and point of view, it also takes the risk of being controversial.

Luxury, like art, is an emotional business. It is one of the few businesses that leaves room for, even indulges and encourages the subjective and irrational. Creating luxury is itself an art form. In that, it is the business that is closest to the human condition. But unlike art, luxury is a celebration. Works like Ai Weiwei's provide a harsh commentary, and so art can focus on a dark vision of reality. On the other hand, luxury recognizes that taking a holistic view does not negate the importance of beauty and sensual pleasure. Luxury holds out hope for a better future.

The machinery that has grown up around today's luxury brands may be coldly calculated finance, merchandising, and marketing. But desire does not follow algorithms. And luxury does not come from the opinions of focus groups. They can only give us their feedback on what already exists, whereas luxury is in the business of constructing ideals. Luxury depends on much more nuanced, sensitive, and unproven methods. These are key to luxury's ability to surprise, delight, and dazzle by exceeding our expectations, by having a point of view and taking risk. In a sense, this is the true rarity of luxury. Not just rare in its quantity, but rare within the range of our experiences. Surprising, delightful, and dazzling are not common currency. To consistently provide them takes ingenuity and a vision of what could be.

For this reason, like art, luxury is a dialogue between the creator and the audience. No other category of consumer brands does this. A consumer may have a preferred brand of toothpaste, but the phrase will always be "honey, please pass me the toothpaste," never "honey, please pass me the Colgate." People will say "my blue shirt," never "my blue Van Heusen." On the other hand, "Who are you wearing?", Joan Rivers' famous question to celebrities on the red carpet, makes perfect sense to us. People regularly refer to "my Birkin," "my Jag," "my Louboutins," "my Mac," rather than referring to the bag, car, shoes, or laptop generically. The same way that a Picasso is always a Picasso. The brand name with the "my" qualifier is a testament to the level of appropriation that people project onto luxury brands, and the brand's ability to maintain its identity even while being appropriated. As in any dialogue, both parties are transformed by the relationship. So, while the user may integrate the brand or product into their lifestyle, because the luxury product retains its identity even as a possession, it exerts an influence on its owner. It changes their perceptions of themselves and therefore their behavior. There is a pride in the object that translates into a sense of self-awareness and self-esteem. But this can only happen if the object is sufficiently significant and respected.

When a brand goes after rapid growth, it runs two risks. First, it is exposed to pressure to do whatever the customer wants. This is a particular problem in fashion, but the fashion cycle has now contaminated other parts of luxury, such as accessories, jewelry, even home décor, which are being pushed to churn out multiple seasonal collections. It started with customers coming into the store asking to see what is new. The desire to meet this demand for novelty took fashion houses beyond designing collections just two seasons a year, to creating bridge collections between seasons, such as cruise and resort collections, as well as capsule collections for specific markets and promotions, which all compete for the time, attention, and resources of creative directors, studios, workshops, suppliers, and so on. They do not have sufficient means to execute the brand's vision through its product properly. Meanwhile, the fashion journalists, buyers, and even customers become so exhausted and jaded by the proliferation of choice that they lose interest. Quality and substance lose out to quantity, the product becomes meaningless, and the dialogue breaks down.

Sometimes, it is literally a breakdown. Suzy Menkes, now international editor for *Vogue*, previously editor for the *International Herald Tribune*, describes an ever accelerating "fashion treadmill," which she points to as being partly behind "the decline of John Galliano, the demise of Alexander McQueen," referring to the former's substance abuse and the latter's suicide.[4] The Galliano incident, in particular, was an interruption of the dialogue between the brand and the customer. Following Galliano's anti-Semitic rant, which had gone viral on social media, Dior were put in the position of having to do damage limitation, while even Natalie Portman, actor and the brand's celebrity representative, spoke out against the designer.[5] Suddenly, the product, no matter how meaningful, takes a back seat to the scandal. Both the Dior and Alexander McQueen brands were able to recover from their respective crises, but for weeks, news about the brands focused on the negative celebrity story rather than the positive associations of the product.

Second, the need for volume causes the brand to lose respect for the object. For example, French luxury brands, part of whose reputation is staked on being made in France, have expanded their production to Italy, Spain, Eastern Europe, even China and Vietnam to meet the volumes and efficiencies required of global business. Suddenly, the French label is more about having been conceived in France, and even then, perhaps by an American or British designer. While this is a natural consequence of globalization, the origin of what it means to be a French luxury brand suddenly becomes an abstraction. The headquarters are in France, but what about the rest? This forces luxury brands to create elaborate stories meant to deliver meaning the product itself no longer carries. The brand becomes a pageant of imagery that celebrates the brand's reflection of itself rather than creating and communicating the meaning of the product. They lose the concrete audience interface of product, and the dialogue becomes monologue.

L'Odyssée de Cartier is a beautiful, animated, short film produced by the brand in 2012, in which a jeweled panther comes to life and explores a surreal landscape that spans Russia, China, India, and Paris. It hits all the brand codes as well as all the cultural clichés. It tells the story of what the brand has been, but gives no indication that the brand has a unique view of the world, nor does it give any indication of where the brand is going – except, perhaps, to the same emerging markets as every other luxury brand. In contrast, in *Hermès Fingerskate*, a live action film by Alexis Milant, a hand skateboards through an urban landscape constructed of Hermès products and packaging. The products are given meaning as the background to a person living their life, not as something to be held central and sacred. Both films magnify the product to superhuman scale. But while Cartier's dominates the landscape, in the Hermès film, for the magnification to work, you must also magnify the hand into a full-sized person. This reflects the Hermès philosophy that the object is meant to integrate so completely into your life that it disappears, placing the emphasis on the individual. The Cartier film is institutional, monumental, speaking from a pinnacle to a massed audience. It is an address, a monologue. The Hermès film, perhaps partly because of its amateur style and technical imperfections, creates intimacy and dialogue. A brand needs both kinds of communication. When it communicates only as an institution, it risks losing the audience's buy-in, especially at a time when consumers are more wary of overly manufactured brand image and more consciously aware of their own desires rather than those being fed to them by marketers.

Cultural critics point out how a disconnect between brand and audience is happening with art. Camille Paglia, author, scholar, and social critic, writes: "Unfortunately, too many artists have lost touch with the general audience and have retreated to an airless echo chamber."[6] Similar criticism has been levied against luxury brands for having retreated from their original positions of leadership and innovation into the insular world of glamour, fashion, and celebrity. And while luxury brands increasingly rely on modern art to demonstrate contemporary relevance, the end result is that the two fields are only reinforcing their sequestration. As they get further removed from real-world interaction, they get separated from the inspiration that comes from the exchange of ideas. Art loses out to popular culture as a social influencer. And luxury cedes its leadership position, reduced to just so much expensive product. As they lose stature, they grasp for attention in other ways. Art critics complain of the endless stream of contemporary pieces that offer little more than the shock value of eroticism or desecration of religious images with excrement. Luxury pursues its own excesses with publicity grabbing baubles such as a $10,000 gold-plated Xbox video game console available at Harrods or the *History Supreme*, a $4.5 billion gold and platinum covered yacht by designer Stuart Hughes. Despite the allusion to timelessness in the yacht's name and despite the artistic ambitions, gestures such as these look increasingly like an extravagant lashing out rather than the true creative genius that gets incorporated into human posterity. Beyond the original media blitz, they do not stand even the shortest test of time before falling into anonymity or even derision. If luxury products lose the intellectual respect of worldly elites, so will the brands that make them. And the long tail of aspirational customers will fall away.

From labor to art

Most brands are content with revisiting old concepts and jumping on fashion trends. But an abstract and fragmented world calls for leadership. This has two important implications for luxury. First, luxury brands, at the top of their league, must lead. Second, like luxury, leadership is an art form. In his book, *Linchpin: Are You Indispensable?*, Seth Godin, a leading thinker on management and marketing, provides a compelling description of how any job can be turned into the making of art.[7] In mechanics, a linchpin is the crucial piece that keeps parts of a complex machine together. In management speak, it is a person who is a pivotal part of an organization. While this function might be easy to define in a machine, the shifting dynamics of an organization mean that the linchpin has to be a good listener, a creative thinker, and a rapid adapter. A linchpin cannot afford to ossify in a fixed vision of their role. They have to look forward and anticipate what is coming. Thus, a linchpin is a combination of artist and leader. A linchpin, like an artist or a leader, has no map to follow. To be a linchpin takes passion and the willingness to connect with others. They are driven by a sense of purpose, and rewarded by a sense of meaning in their work, which in turn provides fulfillment. This means that, more and more, people are looking to be linchpins.

To flourish, a linchpin needs an environment where they have the autonomy to take responsibility for risks and the criticism that comes with proposing something entirely new and unfamiliar. Because luxury does not follow the rules of other types of business, luxury brands are perfectly placed to provide this kind of environment. Instead, too many companies rely on instruction, evidence, and rational arguments, anything that will reassure them with pre-existing proof of their future success. But what has worked in the past or for another luxury brand will almost certainly not work again. Tom Ford and Domenico De Sole were able to orchestrate a spectacular revival of the Gucci brand in the late 1990s. But Bally, which tried to follow the Gucci model, did not have the same effect. For one thing, Bally and Gucci drew on different origins of heritage, biography, and affiliation, which means they need different routes to contemporary relevance. For another, the luxury customer is not looking for multiple replications of the same ideas.

Thus luxury brands are forever challenged to stake new territories with their own unique way of doing things. Luxury firms in their entirety must work like artists and leaders. Luxury brands need linchpins. It is accepted and expected that designers, artisans, artistic directors, even communications and marketing people will work like artists. Now they must be leaders as well. Fashion shows are elaborate theatrical or performance art productions. New product launches are accompanied by highly creative videos, advertising campaigns, and events. But this is not enough. Through their artistic expression they now must contribute to luxury's purpose of engaging in a dialogue with society at large. Like artists, they cannot afford to segregate themselves into a self-congratulatory bubble of glamour and celebrity.

Furthermore, the whole of the organization that supports them must be geared to art and leadership. The administration of luxury – the finance, merchandising, and distribution aspects – is often oriented towards the brand as a business. But, as we said, the market now expects it to be a citizen. Personnel in these roles must have the ability and the authority to look beyond their defined roles and find solutions that support the purpose of the brand. Rather than looking to reinforce the brand by protecting its processes as an institution, they have to be looking for ways to integrate it into the community as a contributor to and leader of values, opinions, and practices. This is where art and leadership become intricately intertwined. Both art and leadership have the responsibility to break new ground. The goal of luxury is to be ahead of its audience.

If established and familiar brands are unable to recognize and respond to this, consumers now have a wealth of new, small, and eager substitutes from which to choose. While big companies struggle to adapt old ways of thinking and working, the competitive threat now comes not from their peers as from an entire universe of agile innovators who have the advantage of incorporating this culture into their mission, process, and communications right from the start. Smaller, niche, and local brands now have access to a global customer base thanks to information and e-commerce technology. Large established brands must compete with these new players for market share. This is especially true for luxury brands, which compete not just for consumers, but specifically for consumers who want to distinguish themselves from the herd. They are subject to the Veblen effect, which eventually drives luxury customers away from brands that are too present. The value of a luxury brand for these customers is not in the weight of popular endorsement, but in their own ability to claim to have discovered something rare and unique. They are less motivated by the tried and trusted, and more willing to trust their own instincts in taking a risk on the unknown. Discovery gives the consumer status linked to knowledge, and the opportunity to establish a personal connection with a brand that is not already surrounded by a mass of followers. It helps them feel like they were part of the process of introducing that brand to the world.

The challenge for luxury brands, then, is to find the true art in their work. This means that they must develop a nuanced understanding of the world. Not just its economic and retail trends, but a sociological and psychological understanding of human behavior – our changing notions of value and success, our evolving ambitions and fears. It is the behavior that creates the trends. Luxury brands must then use this understanding to propose a vision of the world, not just of themselves. Luxury brands have struggled with this last part in particular. They have put so much emphasis on guarding their precious reputations that they have most often chosen to play it safe, relying on old formulas, but becoming less and less impressive or compelling in the process. They trade on product, but in a world of ideas, that will not last much longer. To be sure, this means going out on a limb, exposing oneself to critique and counterarguments. It also means being able to admit when they get it wrong and being grateful for the learning opportunity. This is true innovation, true leadership, true art. It has always been the key to business success. In a world where everyone is expected to lead, and where everyone is becoming an artist, it is now utterly imperative.

Notes

1   www.nowness.com/about.

2   Crabbe, M. and Corlett, D. (2013) "Eroticising inequality: Pornography, young people and sexuality?" Australian Institute of Family Studies seminar, April.

3   Gilsdorf, B. (2010) "Ai Weiwei: Dropping the urn." *Dailyserving*, July 31.

4   Menkes, S. (2013) "Sign of the times: The new speed of fashion." *T Magazine*, August 23.

5   White, B. (2011) "Dior ambassador Natalie Portman speaks out on Galliano." *The Telegraph*, March 1.

6   Paglia, C. (2012) "How capitalism can save art." *The Wall Street Journal*, October 5.

7   Godin, S. (2010) *Linchpin: Are You Indispensable?* Piatkus.

chapter 5

Toward a socially valuable business

- To effectively respond to social pressure and become more responsible, businesses must get away from the box-ticking mentality of compliance and aim for new forms of value creation.

- Shared value is a quantum leap from corporate social responsibility by focusing on the interests that a business has in common, rather than in competition, with the needs of its community.

- Luxury brands' cultural influence allows them to expand the domains for shared value creation, which cements their leadership and aspirational status.

In London, in the spring of 2012, jeweler Fabergé held a charity event called The Big Egg Hunt. It was a citywide Easter egg hunt that followed the opening of the brand's new flagship boutique and coincided with Queen Elizabeth II's diamond jubilee. Artists, designers, and celebrities were invited to design one of over 200 fiberglass eggs, which were then placed around central London. Those who found an egg could send a text message with its location, which served as an entry to win the Fabergé Diamond Jubilee Egg, a bejeweled rose gold egg valued at over £100,00

($150,000). At the end of the 40-day hunt, the designed eggs were sold at auction. Net proceeds from the auctions and text messages went to support two charities – Action for Children and Elephant Family – with the goal of raising £1 million ($1.5 million) for each.[1]

The Fabergé Big Egg Hunt would seem an ideal example of a luxury brand's social responsibility. The combination of Fabergé – famous for the jeweled Easter eggs favored as gifts by the Russian royal family – with an Easter egg hunt and a royal celebration could not be better aligned. The participation of renowned creative professionals, like the Chapman Brothers, Diane von Furstenberg, Zaha Hadid, and Ridley Scott, and famous figures, such as Prince Charles and the Duchess of Cornwall, established reference points between the event and multiple cultural and artistic disciplines. Leveraging technology and supporting a worthy cause put the effort in line with contemporary trends of individual engagement and the desire of people to contribute to good in the world. Finally, the target amounts for contribution to the charities were dazzling.

In the end, about 12,000 people participated in The Fabergé Big Egg Hunt, setting a world record, and all the eggs were sold at auction. Press coverage of the hunt and associated events, like the auctions, glamorous launch parties, and the debut of the Diamond Jubilee Egg prize, drew considerable attention to Fabergé, as the brand was relaunched after a century of decline following the Russian Revolution. But the final amount raised for charity was around £1 million ($1.5 million) in total – still a fortune, but only half the target Fabergé had announced at the launch.[2] Elephant Family's precursor event, the 2010 Elephant Parade, had raised four times as much for just the single charity.[3] The 2013 Big Egg Hunt was decidedly more subdued, sponsored by chocolatier Lindt, rather than by a luxury brand, garnering much less publicity, supporting only one of the charities, Action for Children, and including only half as many eggs.[4] The 2014 edition saw Fabergé replicating its original event in New York.

The great initiative, but debatable outcome of The Fabergé Big Egg Hunt provides a classic example of what happens when a company's business and social responsibility are not sufficiently aligned. The event provided a windfall donation to the charities, but a smaller one than was intended and with no lasting relationship of collaboration and support by the brand or its stakeholders. Indeed, Elephant Family had done better on its own. Further, the event created a one-time burst of publicity for Fabergé that was difficult to recreate in subsequent years. Press coverage of the New York event was far below the level Fabergé achieved in London and around the world in 2012.

While the design of The Fabergé Big Egg Hunt was stylistically perfect, it failed to align very different aims. The two charities, Action for Children and Elephant Family, exist to serve their respective missions of helping children from disadvantaged communities in the UK and protecting an endangered species. But what is the connection between Fabergé and endangered elephants? And while the link between children and an Easter egg hunt is obvious, what is the link between an event designed to engage the British public and the global luxury customer that Fabergé targets? Further, what is the link between the two charities and why split the donation between them? The list of questions could go on and on, applied to the selection of egg designers and other partners who contributed their names and resources to the event. Despite the collaborative effort, each partner sought to leverage their involvement for their own ends. Naturally, the charities were in it for the money. For Fabergé, it was a PR tool. Individual participants were motivated either by the chance to win an expensive prize or purchase an artwork by a famous person.

The shortcoming is in the gap between all these actions and intentions, which delivered fragmented value to the different participants rather than a single, deeper pool of value shared among them. Because there was no natural synergy, the actions of one party did not necessarily amplify those of the others. The Fabergé Big Egg Hunt illustrates the classic levers used in corporate social responsibility (CSR), but they only share coincidence rather than synergy, and the whole adds up to less than the sum of its parts. With no connection between the philanthropic effort and Fabergé's core business, there is no way to calculate whether this effort contributed any value to the company beyond the advertising equivalent of the publicity it garnered. Whether that publicity was effective in contributing to the company's performance we will never know.

There is pressure now for companies to change the way they do business and participate in social issues. There is market pressure from consumers who are increasingly looking behind the product to support companies that behave in accordance with their own values. There is legal pressure stemming from new laws and regulations that ensure companies act honestly, equitably, and responsibly. There is even financial pressure, emerging from investors who understand the importance of exercising long-term vision over pursuing short-term profits. And there is competitive pressure from the myriad new firms enabled by IT to supply a worldwide market with alternatives to established products and brands.

Businesses have been responding. They have improved their corporate governance structures and compliance mechanisms. They are shifting responsibility up the management ladder and the value chain so that new policies have the authority and reach to be effective. Businesses have also raised the profile of sustainability and CSR, in their messaging as well as in their operations. They are explaining the value of these initiatives to their customers, their employees, and their shareholders to create a sense of solidarity behind these objectives. At this point, the website of almost any multinational corporation has extensive information about their efforts and reporting about their accomplishments in this sphere. A universe of consultants has developed to help companies identify their opportunities, improve their performance in these areas, and measure their impacts and the returns on their investments.

But the ability of business to succeed in these efforts stems from how they view the combination of profitability and purpose, and how they pursue value creation and social responsibility. Conducting business responsibly carries a cost. This fact should not be overlooked because that cost raises a barrier to implementation. It makes it more difficult for stakeholders to agree on the ways forward. In the zero-sum world of business thinking, it also means diverting resources from other needs and activities. Furthermore, the ability or even the desire to favor long-term goals over short-term wins is not universally shared. Different stakeholders have different objectives even within their groups. Some investors prefer to buy and hold a steadily growing asset. Others want to reap quick profits and move on to something else. This makes setting objectives, let alone implementing policies and programs, complicated and threatens even the most promising initiatives.

Take environmental protection and climate change, for example. The 2009 UN Climate Change Conference, known as COP15, failed to produce the legally binding international agreement that had been expected to help limit the emission of greenhouse gasses. In the lead-up to the conference, leaked emails exchanged by climate scientists cast doubt on the evidence for global warming. This scandal aside, developing countries resisted pressure to implement controls on greenhouse gas emissions because it would hinder the industrial production on which they depend for economic growth. This argument is an echo of the position expressed by businesses even in developed countries, which argue that the costs of environmental protection threaten to undermine the viability of their business models. In the end, a very watery accord, with no legal bite, was issued by COP15, expressing vague agreement on broad objectives, but nothing that would lead to concrete action. The subsequent annual meetings achieved little more than agreements to make future agreements and the extension of deadlines for meeting objectives that had already been agreed. In November 2013, at COP19, 132 developing countries, led by China, pulled out of the negotiations altogether. The point of fracture was their demands that wealthy countries compensate them for the costs of preventing climate change, not to mention the costs of the damage that had historically come from the developed world.

The same arguments come up with every effort to act in the public interest, be it environmental concerns, improving labor conditions, the equitable distribution of economic gains throughout society, protecting national industries, and so on. On a personal level, we may agree that these are worthwhile aims, but at what cost? How much are we willing to give to achieve them? Companies lobby aggressively against such regulations so that they can protect their economic interests. Shareholders keep a watchful eye on the use of company resources to make sure that their returns on investment are not being squandered. Employees seek to please their corporate masters by "making the numbers." And consumers want the widest possible selection of products at the lowest possible price. Something has to give. Or does it?

New thinking, arising from the growing awareness and sensitivity that people have toward all-around wellbeing, is helping ideas about business value and social value to converge. Michael Porter and Mark Kramer, at Harvard Business School, have introduced the notion of "creating shared value," in which companies seek to do well by also doing good in the world.[5] Instead of focusing on trying to get a bigger piece of the pie, this approach focuses on trying to make the whole pie bigger. In a similar vein, social entrepreneurship is gaining traction, both as a business model and as a legal status for companies in many countries. On the opposite end of the business– social spectrum, legal systems are increasingly allowing nonprofit organizations to conduct for-profit activities in order to decrease their reliance on government and charitable funding while doing their community-focused work.

But all these dynamics are still poorly organized and implemented. For one, there is confusion in people's and companies' thinking about the objectives, design, and achievements of their efforts. Few have gotten their heads around how to create shared value, which is a quantum leap beyond the existing approaches. The picture is muddled further by companies that feel pressured to demonstrate action in these areas, either to enhance their reputations or to seize new market opportunities, but without integrating the necessary values into their corporate culture. This creates skepticism and cynicism around the whole endeavor, tarnishing even those companies that pursue these aims authentically. In the politically polarized environment that emerged from the 2008 economic crisis, talking about business value and social value also enflames debates around capitalism versus socialism, and the appropriate distribution of wealth throughout society.

Terminology like corporate governance, compliance, sustainability and social responsibility, even philanthropy and community engagement are used in interchangeable and often inconsistent ways. In truth, however, these terms are structured into an organized taxonomy. They form a spectrum that goes from a narrow focus to a broad focus (Figure 5.1). The direction in which a company moves through this hierarchy is important. It is an indicator, not just of its responsibility, but of its ability to innovate and its relationship with its market and community. It defines the company's approach to value creation. It speaks to the honesty of its intentions. It will determine if the brand is a leader or a follower. When you understand the big picture, establishing policies, strategies, and practices becomes simple, almost automatic. But when the effort begins with practices that realize only a vague understanding of the big picture, the result is cobbled together and can lack coherence. In this situation, it takes a crisis before an organization begins to consciously think about aligning its actions to its intentions.

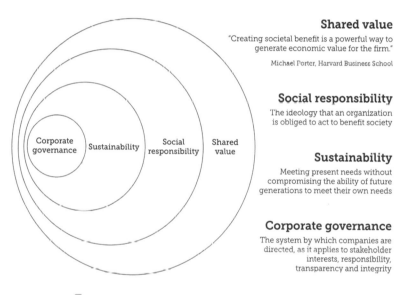

Shared value

"Creating societal benefit is a powerful way to generate economic value for the firm."

Michael Porter, Harvard Business School

Social responsibility

The ideology that an organization is obliged to act to benefit society

Sustainability

Meeting present needs without compromising the ability of future generations to meet their own needs

Corporate governance

The system by which companies are directed, as it applies to stakeholder interests, responsibility, transparency and integrity

FIGURE 5.1 / From governance to creating shared value

This can be a particular challenge for luxury firms. They are often associated with self-indulgence, even selfish extravagance. Their transformation from independent groups into multinational conglomerates has further complicated things. They are beholden to financiers and the same pressures exerted on other firms. The growth imperative means that they have chased after ever larger markets, often pandering to the extremes of materialist excess. By fulfilling their role as the harbinger of good times and the life of the party, they can seem detached from, even indifferent to, more important issues. At the same time, they have innate qualities, such as their respect for the rare and precious, and their proximity to human emotion, which can be tremendous strengths in these areas. The question is how they can seize the opportunity. Porter and Kramer focus on the functional aspects of creating shared value. They look at how a company's processes can be beneficial for the communities in which they are present. But this ignores the power of brands, especially luxury brands, as communications platforms and cultural forces in defining what carries value, creating desire, and shaping consumers' behaviors. Luxury brands' excellence and aspirational qualities, their role as leaders, and their relationship with leaders are particularly potent for creating examples that have a viral influence on individuals and other types of businesses. This points to a new kind of shared value creation, which makes a fertile environment for ethical, responsible, sustainable business and cements the position of luxury as something to aspire to, not just to own, but to emulate as well.

Compliance, governance and ethics: setting the ground rules

Before we can understand the ideas, we need to understand the vocabulary. The terminology behind responsible business follows a logical hierarchy from compliance to corporate governance, ethics, sustainability, social responsibility, and, finally, the creation of shared value. The direction in which a company moves through this hierarchy will determine the success of its efforts. A company that starts from the box-ticking mentality that defines compliance culture will struggle to create shared value because its actions will always be dictated by the demands placed on it from outside. It will always be steps behind the times in understanding and responding to the value expectations of its stakeholders. It will constantly be fending off crises and its actions will be a jumble designed to get away with doing as little as it can. A company that begins from a culture of shared value creation, however, is actively engaged with its external world and thinking proactively about its contribution to that world. It is not just responding to value expectations but helping to shape them as it goes along. While it will not completely avoid making mistakes, the esteem and trust it enjoys will help mitigate the risks, not least because the actions that lead to shared value far exceed the legal minimum required by compliance.

The law provides a foundation for appropriate corporate behavior. And compliance is nothing more than respecting the letter of the law. Companies rightly put a lot of effort into compliance. They employ vast armies of lawyers and technical experts charged with ensuring that they follow the necessary rules and regulations for their business. Compliance is also the underpinning of sound risk management. From a communications standpoint, companies report heavily on their compliant behavior and use it to reinforce their reputation as a trustworthy and reliable brand. But since compliance is nothing more than obeying the law, it really should not even merit discussion from a reputation point of view because, without compliance, companies are simply at the margins of legality. When a company trumpets that they operate within pollution regulations, refuse to use child or forced labor, or promote equal opportunity in the workplace, this is no reason for praise. At best, we can nod in acknowledgement and breathe a sigh of relief. Barbara Pachter, business writer and career consultant, says that one should never use the phrase "I'll be honest with you" because, in effect, it casts doubt on the truth of everything you said up to that point.[6] Without compliance, companies cannot be considered legitimate businesses. The sad fact, however, is that trust in corporations is so low, so much corporate behavior is assumed to be at or beyond the margins of legality, that a statement of compliance does have value. Compliance is about respecting the letter of the law, not the spirit of the law, and companies often get caught exploiting loopholes in, say, tax, labor, or environmental regulations with complete impunity. That we have accepted business culture's decay to such a state is a sorry commentary on the business values at work today, and the values that individuals accept to uphold when they go into work.

Corporate governance is a form of compliance. This is the next level in the hierarchy. Corporate governance is the system by which companies are directed, as it applies to stakeholders' interests, responsibility, transparency, and integrity. It addresses issues such as ownership, control and decision-making structures, financial reporting, auditing of a company's accounts and operations systems, and even narrow issues such as executive pay. There is no one universal system of corporate governance. International agreements on corporate governance include standards put forward by the International Corporate Governance Network, the OECD Principles of Corporate Governance and its Guidelines for Multinational Enterprises. The OECD's 1997 Anti-Bribery Convention makes it illegal for corporate officers to bribe foreign government officials. Within these, countries take different approaches to corporate governance based on their respective legal and cultural traditions. These rules apply particularly as a condition for listing a firm on stock exchanges. Some European countries mandate a two-tier board of directors that separates operational management and oversight functions. The US and UK models are designed to safeguard the investments and rights of shareholders first. With time, corporate governance practices have become better organized and regimented. In the wake of a series of high-profile corporate bankruptcies in the early 2000s, including the Enron and WorldCom collapses, the US introduced the Sarbanes-Oxley Act in 2002, which gave more responsibility to CEOs for a company's finances and set more stringent standards for auditing and managing conflicts of interest. Corporate governance is, however, little more than a way to ensure compliance and enhance the management of risk. From an ethical perspective, corporate governance is mostly neutral. The Securities and Exchange Board of India is one of the few bodies that makes reference to corporate governance as a tool for ethical business conduct. Mostly, it is there to ensure that the company does not misbehave. Beyond that, it carries no obligation.

Derived from corporate governance policies are company codes of conduct, business practice and ethics. At this level, we begin to see the expression of a corporate culture, values, and expectations in terms of behavior and relationships between people. Depending on the company, these documents carry varying importance for the organization. They are often rule books that spell out the dos and don'ts of maintaining company confidentiality, the use of company resources, the management of interpersonal disputes and conflicts of interest, and the protection of employees from harassment and discrimination, among other issues. They can go further, explaining a company's attitude toward and definitions of fair and ethical business practices. In some organizations, these codes form an integral part of a new hire's orientation. More often than not, however, they are simply slipped into the package of documents handed to newly arrived employees and available for reference on internal websites. They may be used as the basis for workshops on issues such as sexual harassment and inclusive management. Codes of conduct and ethics are frequently developed in response to a specific crisis or conflict, and then live on as theoretical guides. References to treating employees with respect, appropriate language, and attitude, and suggestions for conflict resolution come across as nice ideas in an ideal world. The danger is that they end up forgotten, ignored or, worse, regarded with cynicism by a company's employees. Finally, they are innately internal documents, frequently developed by the human resources and legal departments. This removes them a few steps from the management of the company's brand and the culture that emanates from the leadership style of the top executives. When these guides represent ideal-world scenarios and risk management needs of human resource and legal departments, they can create a schism between external appearance and internal experience. We have all experienced the cliché: fun and friendly on the outside, while inside, it is politics, palace intrigue, and *The Devil Wears Prada*.[7]

Sustainability: from rules to ambitions

The ethics of business come into focus with the inclusion of sustainability. Defined broadly, sustainability means meeting present obligations without compromising the ability of future generations to meet their own needs. Classic sustainability thinking encompasses three pillars – environmental, social, and economic – with some pundits having more recently added a cultural pillar. The environmental pillar has been the most common entry point for companies in developing a sustainability agenda. Public pressure took an early interest in the environmental impacts of businesses, from air, water and ground pollution, the consumption of water and other natural resources such as paper products and energy, to protecting wilderness areas and biodiversity. Legal systems were quick to take up measures that protect the environment from harm, including protecting air quality, water supplies, sensitive ecosystems, and endangered species. Companies were required to adapt, cleaning up their materials processing, waste treatment and disposal, and being more careful about their sourcing of materials and fuels. As recycling gained popularity, companies also improved their sourcing and disposal of paper products. More recently, they have been working to increase their use of clean and renewable energy to power their factories, offices, and vehicles. The focus on environmental performance ahead of the social pillar stems from the availability of clearer, more concrete, and more objectively measurable deliverables. Further, energy and material efficiencies bring benefits by lowering consumption and the associated costs.

In 2011, PUMA and parent company PPR (since renamed Kering), published their first environmental profit and loss account (EP&L).[8] The first of its kind, the report sought to quantify PUMA's environmental impact by looking at the whole of their operations and supply chain, and allowed the company to measure their environmental performance in financial terms. The EP&L calculated PUMA's environmental impact at €145 million, concentrated in their water use, greenhouse gas emissions, land use, air pollution and waste. It also showed most of these impacts coming from their supply chain in Asia and tier 4 suppliers, the furthest ring out in their value chain. This information empowered PUMA to target future sustainability efforts on specific regions and activities, and signaled to the company that they needed to make more effort to work with upstream suppliers in meeting their sustainability standards. The product-level EP&L allowed PUMA to calculate differences in environmental impact between examples of their standard and more sustainable products, which helped the company understand whether their sustainability initiatives were having a real, positive effect on the environment. With the completion of the first corporate-level EP&L, Kering announced their plan to implement the audit across all the luxury, sport and lifestyle brands that they own by 2015. Also in 2011, building on sustainability initiatives that had begun in 2000, Kering put in place a corporate sustainability team with technical and change management expertise, reporting to the CEO and integrated into a network of interlocutors throughout the entire company, in every subsidiary and at every management and operational level. Kering also announced a set of group-wide sustainability targets. These include eliminating the use of hazardous chemicals by 2020, and by 2016: eliminating the use of PVC; reducing emissions, waste, and water use by 25 percent; sourcing 100 percent of paper and packaging, precious skins, leather, fur, gold and diamonds sustainably and humanely; and auditing key suppliers a minimum of every two years.[9]

Environmental sustainability, as both a legal requirement and a financial advantage, can be an easier win for firms than the more diffuse and complex terrain of social sustainability. On the social side, examples of initiatives include looking after fair labor and wage practices and working conditions, developing a demographically diverse workforce, and ensuring that human rights are respected all along the value chain. These areas are, however, often already covered by compliance practices, unless a company chooses to operate at a standard above that which local law requires of them. In practice, this has been rare. When companies expand production into lower cost labor markets, they are specifically seeking to benefit from the disparity with their home market on issues such as minimum employment age, working hours, and benefits. To have a company-wide standard based on the practices required at headquarters and apply it at the same level globally would make little sense. So, even in these quite objective areas, we often see the same company working to different criteria in different countries. The best among them will extend their value system and management culture, adapted to the local context.

Social sustainability sees people, like the environment, as a finite resource that must be nurtured and protected. Madeleine Vionnet (1876–1975) founded her haute couture fashion house in Paris in 1912. In the early part of the 20th century, Vionnet's social practices far exceeded the standards of the day. Most of the benefits enjoyed by employees today, such as healthcare for themselves and family members, paid maternity leave, and financial assistance, were already extended to workers in her company by the 1920s. According to Vionnet:

> This is all completely normal … and not worth discussing. We shouldn't overlook anything to promote and protect health because you have to be in very good health to successfully work in the couture trade.[10]

Vionnet's approach was formed by her experience as a linen maid at the Holloway Sanatorium in London and the practices she observed during her subsequent career with couture houses, which allowed the behavior of their sales teams to dictate their products and corporate culture. Vionnet executed a vision of an ideal company that would revolutionize both fashion and working conditions. As a feminist, she worked to create the simpler, more functional garments that liberated women were looking for, and used fabric technology to introduce the revealing bias cut that would come to define the feminine silhouette of the Art Deco period. She built a factory with large windows, where the typical seamstress stools were replaced with ergonomically designed sewing stations. Heating and ventilation systems were run from the basement to keep the air in the ateliers pure. She was the first to provide her staff with paid leave, which would not become a legal requirement in France for over a decade. Medical staff provided free care to workers as well as their parents on site, so as to maintain updated records and save the time lost traveling to and from doctors appointments. Childcare was provided, as was a fund for the newborn children of workers. Employees also benefited from a retirement fund. And yet, Vionnet was clear that she was not running a social service, but a business that needed to produce and sell at a profit. She saw social sustainability as one part of efficiency. At its height, Vionnet & Cie employed 1,200 people, making it the largest couture house in Paris, even larger than Chanel. Although the company suffered during the Great Depression, it was only closed with the coming of

World War II. The brand built by a girl born to a poor family in rural France was revived in 2006, and since 2009 Vionnet Paris have been headquartered in Milan. Whether the new owner of the brand, an heiress and former investment banker from Kazakhstan, will be able to follow through on the execution of Vionnet's vision remains to be seen.

The last pillar of sustainability, the economic pillar, is the continued viability of the business alongside its commitments in the environmental and social areas. Little has been said about economic sustainability because it is considered the default position of business, looking after its own needs. Indeed, what has been said occasionally disparages a business for continuing to profit and grow while touting environmental and/or social issues. Writing about Patagonia, the maker of high-performance outerwear, business journalist Kyle Stock called the company's marketing "sanctimonious" for resulting in double-digit sales growth while imploring consumers to buy less.[11] But this assessment is stuck in the mindset that doing good and doing well are innately incompatible. If consumers reward a company for its ethical stance, why do we find this hypocritical when it is precisely the outcome that sustainability is designed to create?

With the addition of environmental and social considerations, the overriding concern was to not erode the economic pillar too much. Companies aim to pursue sustainability agendas while maintaining similar levels of profitability and growth. To really integrate doing good with doing well, we do need to address the question of "How well?" We need to go the extra step of revising economic performance criteria to take account of the added constraints imposed by social and environmental consciousness. This does not mean ignoring the profit motive, but adopting a healthier, more balanced attitude toward profitability. Environmental and social sustainability have gained traction in business thinking because the logic of long-term returns has finally gained acceptance as business has begun embracing public opinion on these issues. But economic sustainability is still beholden to the pressure of the short-term approaches commonly found in financial markets. Investors may want better behavior from their companies, but they are not prepared to sacrifice returns or growth. To let these lag would be to invite reproach from analysts and shareholders. But an honest look at economic sustainability would not shy away from these controversial topics. It would seek to address issues such as appropriate profit levels, growth rates, and distribution of the gains. Even free-market champions such as the OECD and billionaire George Soros, who founded the Institute for New Economic Thinking, are taking up this challenge and working on defining the parameters of sustainable and inclusive growth.

Social responsibility: from ambitions to intentions

While sustainability is a focus on ensuring long-term returns, social responsibility is the ideology that organizations should act to benefit society. Many people use the two terms interchangeably. Some rank them in a different order. They consider sustainability a step above social responsibility because social concerns are one of the three pillars of sustainability. But this focus on specific issues fails to take in the bigger picture. The social pillar of sustainability seeks to preserve and perpetuate the community as a resource for the firm. Social responsibility, on the other hand, is holistic thinking about the role of the firm in the community and the impacts that it has, both social and environmental. Sustainability can lead to silo thinking about the relationship between the company and the community. It can also pit stakeholders against one another in the allocation of resources, responsibilities, and benefits unless sustainability is seen as part of the business model. Social responsibility seeks to create consensus around these issues – and does not ignore the environmental aspects – in a way that moves society forward as a whole.

Social responsibility grew out of the social movements of the 1960s and 70s, a turning point at which companies had become so large and politically influential that people began to consider their impacts and role beyond just making money. But social responsibility can bring a firm into complex territory. The difficulties that firms encounter in addressing the social pillar of sustainability are magnified when they try to take a more holistic approach to their role in society. It raises questions that strike at the heart of a firm's mission and purpose. For most companies, that is a highly disruptive introspection. More reasonably, however, it can be a guide for reflection on ethical business practices and the true nature of value creation. Social responsibility, when it is pursued authentically, is also a powerful method of brand differentiation and managing reputational and operational risks.

Done right, social responsibility is a form of self-regulation that companies integrate into their business model, so that the costs are accommodated and the benefits are identified and can be measured. The International Standards Organization's 26000 standard for social responsibility was launched in 2010. It guides organizations in recognizing their social responsibility and identifying and engaging stakeholders in its implementation. The ISO 26000 standard focuses on core areas of human rights, labor practices, the environment, fair operating practices, consumer issues, and community involvement and development. It promotes principles of accountability, transparency, ethical behavior, and respect for stakeholder interests, and laws and standards of behavior. The OECD Guidelines for Multinational Enterprises, which were adopted in 1976 and revised every few years since then, address similar issues to the ISO 26000, and also cover combating bribery and respecting the spirit as well as the letter of the law when it comes to competition and taxation. While both documents provide direct guidance to companies, the OECD's guidelines focus more specifically on companies doing business internationally and can help them establish a global baseline of behavior independently of what local regulations may tolerate.

While sustainability focuses attention on a company's actions, operations, and footprint, social responsibility puts it in collaboration with the outside world. And it shifts the emphasis from mitigating damage to actually making a positive impact. For example, companies may look to operate in areas where they have the ability to create previously impossible economic opportunities. They also invest heavily in building facilities for education and medical care. Some work on helping once poor communities adapt to newfound economic prosperity. Because social responsibility can quickly exceed a company's core competences, collaboration with the public and nonprofit sectors is a frequent channel for realizing a company's goals.

Corporate philanthropy is one of the oldest forms of social responsibility. Belief in the importance of corporate philanthropy has existed for a century or more. Andrew Carnegie described the importance of philanthropy in *The Gospel of Wealth* as early as 1889.[12] Since 2000, Louis Vuitton have worked with Sharon Stone and the American Foundation for AIDS Research (amfAR) to produce a line of vanity cases and shoulder bags, the sales of which have raised almost $4 million in support of AIDS research.[13] The link between Louis Vuitton and amfAR is a stylistic one to be sure. Sharon Stone, as amfAR's global fundraising chairman and a movie star, serves as the bridge between the charity and a luxury brand long associated with celebrities and glamorous travel, so a vanity case as the physical incarnation of the partnership makes sense. Superficially, the link between Louis Vuitton and AIDS research is tenuous, and could be seen as arbitrary, not unlike the link between

Fabergé and endangered Asian elephants. On closer examination, however, the origin of the AIDS epidemic in the gay community disproportionately affected people in the creative professions, such as fashion and entertainment. Elizabeth Taylor, the legendary movie star, was amfAR's founding international chairman in 1985 and a celebrity activist for AIDS research at a time when the disease was claiming other iconic figures like actor Rock Hudson, musicians Liberace and Freddy Mercury, and designers Halston and Perry Ellis, but few were willing to speak up for AIDS' victims. Sadly, AIDS became particularly relevant to the worlds of Louis Vuitton and Sharon Stone. This commonality makes it possible to take the collaboration to greater depths – such as by integrating products into the brand's permanent collection outside the capsule of a time-bound campaign – without raising questions of legitimacy.

This illustrates one of the biggest questions regarding CSR initiatives: the appropriateness of the cause to which a company's resources are committed. Unless the social efforts are linked to a company's business model in some way, philanthropy is the transfer of a company's value to others rather than the creation of value for the community and the firm. It certainly advances the social sustainability agenda overall but, as in the example of Fabergé, it can fail to provide long-term value unless it is integrated into a company's core activities. A privately owned firm such as Fabergé has the freedom to select a cause based on the owners' personal proclivities and affiliations. A public company like LVMH, however, could be criticized by shareholders for channeling what the law considers their money into causes without seeking their prior consent.

Reconciling the diverging interests, lobbying and other forms of activism can be a more sophisticated form of social responsibility, if used correctly. The typical view of corporate lobbying is one of companies pressing government officials to pass laws that create a favorable environment for their business. But examples of the opposite exist. In addition to their work on more familiar aspects of social responsibility, such as sustainable sourcing, Tiffany & Co. have been active in pushing for laws that prevent mining in environmentally and culturally sensitive areas.[14] In 1996, Tiffany & Co. worked with the US Department of the Interior against the opening of a gold mine near Yellowstone National Park. In 2004, the company launched a media campaign against the proposed Rock Creek mine in Montana, which would threaten the region's wildlife and water supply. In 2010, they made a similar awareness-raising effort regarding the Pebble Mine in Bristol Bay, Alaska, committing publicly to never buy gold from the mine if it were to open. Tiffany & Co. are also a founding member of the Responsible Jewellery Council, an industry watchdog founded in 2005, the standards of which most luxury jewelry companies have now endorsed. Other examples exist in the area of animal rights, such as L'Occitane's work to get the Chinese government to repeal laws that require all imported cosmetic and skincare products to undergo animal testing. While some criticize L'Occitane for doing business in China at all under these circumstances, according to the company:

> Unfortunately given the limited economic and political weight of L'Occitane, ceasing to sell our products in China will not do anything to change local regulations. Instead, to move forward we decided to develop our relationship with the Chinese authorities to pledge the case for the ending of animal testing for beauty products, through open dialogue.[15]

The Chinese authorities' agreement to stop testing sun care products on animals is a first sign of the success of L'Occitane's efforts to improve things from within the system rather than by boycotting the market. Luxury brands have also been active in the promotion of intellectual property rights, which not only protect their designs but also the future of artisanal professions that are forever under threat by industrialization and outsourcing.

The hell of good intentions

Despite the wealth of initiatives, the marriage between business and social responsibility is fraught with difficulty. Companies that have recognized the positive effects for their brand image have been quick to adopt sustainability messaging and practices without fully integrating the approach into their business process. The biggest shortcoming is that there is often a large gap between their lofty ideals and realizable, on-the-ground action. The UN Global Compact's *Global Corporate Sustainability Report 2013* found that 65 percent of companies were developing policies at senior executive levels, but only 35 percent showed any meaningful action as a result.[16] The credibility of sustainability and social responsibility initiatives is further undermined by the propensity of companies to use them for PR and goodwill, without genuine interest in the underlying philosophies. This can create some odd situations. One example is organic foods. When industrial food companies recognized the market potential of organic produce, they were quick to develop product lines in response while lobbying governments to lower the bar on what could be labeled "organic," thus debasing the credibility of the entire sector. The website of Philip Morris International (PMI), the tobacco company, provides detailed information about its sustainability initiatives and performance targets. These include areas of environmental performance, climate change, agricultural practices, helping rural communities, and workplace safety. But even the casual observer would immediately wonder what good these good deeds are doing in the service of a product that, according to the company's own website, causes serious disease and is addictive.[17] PMI, being a publicly listed company, are required to undertake a baseline of sustainability initiatives. They also have a fiduciary responsibility to investors in terms of revenues and growth, which requires them to always seek out new markets. In combining the two, are we to conclude that PMI are, effectively, in the business of sustainable disease and addiction?

The UN Global Compact has tried to bring order to such chaos, identifying ten principles to do with human rights, labor standards, the environment, and anti-corruption. But the Global Compact is not a legally binding agreement. Many critics, including influential figures within the UN, cite the Global Compact as being toothless, having no monitoring or enforcement mechanisms, and subject to manipulation by companies who use it as a smokescreen.[18] Even the UN Global Compact's own actions can sometimes make one wonder. At its 2013 Leadership Summit, UN Secretary-General Ban Ki-moon unveiled a model of the UN headquarters built of over 90,000 of the Lego toy company's nonbiodegradable, virtually indestructible plastic bricks. Lego do identify research into more sustainable alternatives to their current materials as a priority.[19] Meanwhile, Lego highlight their contribution to "sustainable play" through quality toys that can be passed down for generations. However, any parent or anyone who grew up playing with Lego bricks knows that the sets of building blocks disperse over time, constantly releasing millions of the indestructible little plastic pieces into the environment. Although the plastic is recyclable and its durability makes the pieces highly reusable, Lego have not set up an end-of-life recovery process that would allow the bricks to be recycled either as components or a raw material. Consumers have been left to organize themselves via websites like brickrecycler.com to manage the sustainable disposal of Lego bricks. Given these circumstances, while the link between the UN Global Compact summit's theme, "Architects of a Better World," and Lego's focus on "Inspiring and helping children to develop"[20] is a poignant one, did nobody find the photo-op of a giant, plastic toy at a sustainability leadership conference a tad out of place?

The UN Global Compact shows that the sincerest of efforts, if not completely thought through, can easily stumble on the path to environmental awareness. When addressing social issues, they can flirt with the patronizing and even grotesque. In cities such as Rio de Janeiro, Johannesburg, and Mumbai, an industry has developed around guided tours of shantytowns and urban slums. Many of these began as a way to bridge the class divide and allow people to learn about the lives and struggles of the poor. With their growing popularity, however, some have become more of a badge on the chic tourist trail, an elaborate show of sensitivity that actually reduces the residents of these areas to little more than a carnival sideshow. The word is "slumming," an elite pastime that has long been reviled. In places and times with strict class hierarchies, there were social conventions that governed such behavior. Edwardian Britain had well-understood rules that first-class ship passengers did not visit steerage for their personal amusement. Even a lord of the manor knew under precisely what circumstances he was allowed to enter (and apologetically at that) the staff quarters of his own home in order to protect the privacy and dignity of those who lived there. But as social hierarchies have flattened around the world, we have forgotten these conventions and opened the door to transgression.

Now, contact with the poor is not even a prerequisite to learning about the poor. The Shanty Town (Makhukhu Village) at the Emoya Luxury Hotel & Spa in Bloemfontein, South Africa offers a village of corrugated iron cabins, accented with fires burning in open metal drums and billed as "the only Shanty Town in the world equipped with under-floor heating and wireless internet access!"[21] The hotel is proposed as "a Shanty within the safe environment of a private game reserve," a quaint and colorful site for "fancy theme parties." It is reminiscent of Marie Antoinette's hamlet at Versailles, where she would escape the strictures of courtly life to play a peasant girl at a beautifully manicured, fake farmstead. By living out a fantasy of "normal life" in an isolated bubble, Marie Antoinette famously became a symbol of just how far the French ruling elite had gone from understanding the travails of the masses. We know how that story ended.

Creating shared value

CSR and sustainability used to be a matter of "if." With increased public awareness, it is now a matter of "how" and particularly "how much." When Royal Caribbean Cruises Ltd built a school for local children on land they lease from the Haitian government as a beach destination for their ships, detractors were quick to point out that the school's budget was only a tiny fraction of what the company had spent to build a new quay at the same location. While the ships carry enough food for 3,000 passengers to enjoy a week's worth of all-you-can-eat-around-the-clock dining, the school did not provide lunch to the several dozen students who come from malnourished homes and whose parents pay a modest tuition fee for their attendance. While the company acknowledged these shortcomings, John Weis, Royal Caribbean's associate vice president, said: "We have a responsibility to the community... but it's not unlimited."[22] While the company had earned praise for using their ships and facilities to provision Haiti after the devastating earthquake of 2010, there was still a sense that, with $6.8 billion in tax-free revenues, the company could be doing more.

The reason that sustainability and social responsibility initiatives so easily go awry is that the driving values are frequently misguided. With the entirety of business and economic ideals still centered on generating profit and growth, we flail in the effort to integrate broader thinking. But as we discussed in Chapter 4, the world is now quickly pushing us from being self-focused to being self-centered but other-focused. An effort to translate this into the business realm was developed by Michael Porter and Mark Kramer, founders in 2000 of FSG, a nonprofit strategy consultancy. Their "creating shared value" model holds that creating value for society is the way to generate value for the firm.[23] It is a major step beyond CSR (Table 5.1), yet, in a sense, it is a return to the origins of enterprise, where companies exist to create value for customers, only as a result of which do they create value for shareholders. But it takes these origins further by accounting for the complex interdependence of the world we live in today, and thus sees a company's customers as society at large. It recognizes that the market is not separate from society and that the firm is a citizen within that society.

TABLE 5.1 The difference between corporate social responsibility and creating shared value [23]

CSR – Corporate Social Responsibility	CSV – Creating Shared Value
Value: Doing good	Value: Economic and societal benefits relative to cost
Citizenship, philanthropy, sustainability	Joint company and community value creation
Discretionary or in response to external pressure	Integral to competing
Separate from profit maximization	Integral to profit maximization
Agenda is determined by external reporting and personal preferences	Agenda is company specific and internally generated
Impact limited by corporate footprint and CSR budget	Realigns the entire company budget
Example: Fair trade purchasing	Example: Transforming procurement to increase quality and yield

An often cited example of creating shared value is Nestlé's work with dairy farmers in Pakistan. Nestlé Pakistan's Creating Shared Value program focuses on nutrition, water, and rural development. This includes providing milk and nutritionally reinforced products to schools, and helping communities secure access to clean water. The cornerstone of the program is training farmers in practices that help increase the quantity and quality of milk yield, and involving women in the agricultural process. Called the Dairy Project, the goal is to educate 9,000 farmers, 2,000 unemployed local youths, and 5,000 women in practices such as livestock breeding, maintenance, nutrition, and milking.[24] By helping the community, Nestlé are also reinforcing their supply chain for dairy products. The collaboration also carries a price agreement, which ensures stable future costs for the company and reliable future revenues for farmers.

Some have called the creating shared value model little more than a repackaging of existing sustainability and social responsibility approaches. But it does go further in integrating these considerations into the business model of an organization. More importantly, it represents a paradigm shift in the way business thinks about its social value. Under the shared value framework, social value is no longer about limiting negative impacts or offsetting them with giveaways in other domains. It is about proactively seeking to make a positive impact on the outside world in a way that delivers returns to the company. This shift in thinking is crucial. Whether a company moves outward from compliance or inward from shared value creation, the direction will be the determining factor in its future success.

Until now, companies have tended to opt for the easy route: moving to higher levels in response to evolving trends, public pressure, and government regulations. But this puts them perpetually behind the times. Take the example of McDonald's. The rapid expansion of fast food throughout the 1960s and 70s eventually gave rise to concerns about nutrition quality. Until the 1980s, fast-food restaurants like McDonald's were a pleasant convenience; an inexpensive night out, a reassuringly familiar rest stop on a long drive. With the public debate on nutrition and rising obesity levels, McDonald's classic hamburger, French fries and soda model became a source of concern about empty calories and saturated fats. In response, McDonald's introduced their first salads in 1985. In the 1990s and 2000s, environmental issues stole the agenda. These spurred the company to make improvements to their packaging, energy use, and sourcing practices. Styrofoam containers were eliminated in favor of recycled and recyclable paper and cardboard. McDonald's restaurants now send employees on patrols around the neighborhood to clean up litter dropped by their customers. McDonald's have also done more to source ingredients from independent and local farmers, rather than industrial agriculture and food processing companies. More recently, McDonald's have had to respond to attacks on how animals are treated by their suppliers. Then came the uproar about the "pink slime" and "white slime" processed meats used to fill out the volumes of their beef and chicken products. Then there was one about how McDonald's quietly rewarded influential "mommy bloggers" for spreading positive messages about their food.[25] The most recent scandal surrounds providing a living wage for workers in McDonald's restaurants. And during all this, questions about nutritional value and McDonald's contribution to the worldwide obesity epidemic have never gone away, despite a steadily increasing offer of healthy options on their menus.

While all these developments drive McDonald's forward, the company constantly finds themselves behind an evolving issue. Their communications teams constantly have to conduct crisis management. A 2012 social media effort based on themes like #McDStories and #MeetTheFarmers, which was meant to highlight their authentic values with "salt of the earth" messaging, was upended by a tsunami of negative user comments on Twitter, causing the company to shut the campaign down within a matter of hours.[26] While McDonald's are mostly perceived as a fast-food restaurant, at their core, a company like McDonald's feeds people, and provides gathering places, familiarity, and reliable levels of safety and quality. These are noble endeavors. To change their entire brand dynamic, McDonald's only need recognize the nobility in their work. If McDonald's limit their self-image to being a fast-food restaurant, this keeps their nose to the grindstone of daily operations, efficiency, margins, and cost cutting. They will fail to see their true role in the community and the value they could bring, if they chose to. As long as the core product is not a healthy contribution to society, your brand is forever vulnerable to attack. Compliance determines the brand's actions rather than the initiative to create shared value. So, McDonald's remain locked in a methodology that keeps the rod at their back and "love" perpetually out of reach.

On the other hand, truly exemplary companies do not try to shoehorn social value into their business model, but design their business model around the value they want to create. This guides their actions all along the value chain and provides a meaningful, creative challenge rather than a barrier that needs to be overcome or gone around. Patagonia go so far as to tell customers "Don't buy this jacket" in their advertising and on their product tags. As a maker of clothing for the outdoors, they understand the intrinsic link between their commercial success and environmental preservation. Rather than encouraging their customers to buy more products, they encourage their customers to buy products wisely and they help their customers maintain, repair, and recycle them. This means that Patagonia must conceptualize, design, and manufacture their products with an eye toward being able to repair and recycle them in the future, from the choice of fibers to consumer outreach, to providing the necessary after-sales systems.

Many brands create eco-friendly products, but few provide the infrastructure to reabsorb products at the end of their life. In 2005, Patagonia launched the Common Threads program to encourage customers to buy only what they need and what will last, to repair what breaks, to share what they no longer use, and to recycle everything else. This advocacy includes external stakeholders in Patagonia's responsibility agenda of protecting the environment, creating a community, and letting the customer reap the immediate advantages of saving money. On Black Friday 2013, the day after Thanksgiving and the US's biggest shopping day of the year, when most US companies hold sales to break even on the year's accounts, Patagonia organized Worn Wear Parties, with film screenings, repair workshops, and other events that help people "celebrate the stuff you already own." Patagonia's iFixit is a startup that creates repair manuals for Patagonia clothes. This supplements the repair programs that Patagonia have run as a service to customers for years.

Any critic who thinks that discouraging purchases eats into Patagonia's sales should think again. In 2012, which was dominated by the "Buy Less" campaign, revenues increased by a third, demonstrating the powerful potential of shared value creation. According to Patagonia founder Yvon Chouinard:

> I know it sounds crazy, but every time I have made a decision that is best for the planet, I have made money. Our customers know that— and they want to be part of that environmental commitment.[27]

The shared value of luxury

Luxury brands rely on brand love. To appeal to customers who are used to the best, to arouse aspirational desire, to inspire creativity and passion among their designers and artisans, luxury brands must instill respect, pride, and devotion. Yet luxury brands have been slower than others to openly embrace sustainability and social responsibility. In part, this is a matter of complacency with their prior achievements. Luxury brands have a long history of treating rare materials with due care and respect for their preservation. Their artisans are no mere laborers, and luxury brands have always understood that appropriate working conditions are a prerequisite for producing the quality work they require. Luxury brands also have a long history of philanthropy and support for the arts. So, when challenged on their practices, luxury brands can truthfully claim that they have been pursuing sustainability and social responsibility all along. But the world has also moved on. Promoting the arts is a limited view of luxury's role in the world and what it represents to people. In the shift from "if" to "how," luxury brands must not just be supporters, but proactive problem solvers. And they have to make the quantum leap from being responsible businesses to actually creating shared value.

Luxury is seen by many as superfluous, self-indulgent, even excessive. We are often asked how shared value can be derived from something essentially nonessential. But we do not accept this characterization of luxury. We do not accept that the world would tolerate having an estimated two million people dedicated to the futile task of creating something utterly unnecessary. That would surely have been washed away by time and natural selection. Furthermore, even if the world did tolerate it, we do not accept that these two million people are unnecessary, that they consider themselves and their work superfluous, and squander their time and energy in such a way. That may be what the image of luxury has become, but it is not what luxury is about. The challenge is for luxury firms – and by this we mean the people who work within them – to find what is essential about luxury and what is essential about their contribution. When luxury brand managers focus only on the glamorous side of luxury, they are, in effect, diminishing the value of their own work. They are refusing to take ownership of the importance of what they do and shirking their responsibility. They are not going deep enough in their approach or appreciation of the profession. And when they do that, luxury indeed becomes shallow, pandering, and superfluous. It loses its luster. And eventually it will implode.

This leaves luxury firms with a complex dilemma. How do you reconcile public demand for accountability with consumer demand for products and investor demand for profit and growth? How do you motivate teams to reengineer processes and think differently about their work? How do you integrate the growing awareness of communal needs into a value proposition centered on self-indulgence? Shared value is more than just a mechanism like sustainability, or a philosophy like social responsibility. Shared value is a conviction that drives a company to create the most, and most broadly felt, value possible. To look for luxury's shared value, we have to look beyond the product. It has been ages since the product encapsulated the value of a luxury good all by itself. Luxury brands, much more than others, trade on reputation and goodwill. They invest heavily in their visibility and their affiliation with leading social and cultural figures. Luxury's value is thus in the power of combining operations and communications: its content, its messages, its visibility, its desirability, its influence, its unique propensity to steer values and shepherd the crowd. It is in the power to shape people's thinking, values, and behavior by showing them what they should aspire to. Luxury can move the dial.

Luxury can spearhead the business shift toward more responsible and sustainable practices. This new paradigm, despite its clean-living, do-good, feel-good rhetoric, is weighted with a sense of sacrifice and effort, be it in compromised product quality or the burden of resource and operational constraints. At the same time, it is a moving target, always steps ahead of us, and with the most direct benefits going to others, which undermines the feeling of progress, achievement, or reward. The customer in New York, Paris, or Singapore is being asked to make an effort that will benefit an unknown individual either thousands of miles away or three generations into the future. But what does the customer get out of it in the here and now? Luxury's essence is positive, a vision of a better life. Luxury can project a vision of the world as it should be and inspire individual action. It can raise the level of perceived benefits above the level of perceived costs. Luxury firms can make sustainable products desirable. They can release responsible business from its image of compromise and "less than." Consumers accept responsible products only when they do not compromise on design and quality. For mass-market goods, another constraint is price. But luxury customers are less price-sensitive. Indeed, the Veblen goods we defined in Chapter 2 actually become more desirable as price and perceived value rises. So, luxury goods have an opportunity to push the envelope.

Tesla Motors entered the market in 2006 with an all-electric roadster selling for over $125,000. While it received a mixed reception from car enthusiasts, it quickly became a badge of honor, particularly in Hollywood and Silicon Valley, among a set of wealthy trendsetters wanting to make a statement about their commitment to the environment. Its popularity caught on and Tesla subsequently introduced their Model S sedan and Model X sport utility vehicle. The company also collaborated with Smart, Mercedes-Benz, Toyota, and Freightliner on more accessible models and vans. Having thus developed trust in and demand for electric vehicles, in late 2013, Tesla announced their intention to launch a low-priced car to compete in the mass market.

Beyond more familiar sustainability, we find opportunities even more closely aligned with luxury's unique strengths and where it can have a greater impact. Developed countries that are home to luxury brands are rapidly deindustrializing as manufacturing jobs are outsourced to emerging economies. The consequent loss of employment opportunities will continue to challenge countries' economic performance by putting pressure on public finances and social welfare systems. In part, the job loss is due to consumer demand for ever less expensive products and shareholder demand for ever higher margins. But it also stems from the perception of manufacturing as low-value, low-differentiated work, easily substituted at lower price points. In truth, manufacturing requires skills that take time to develop, learn, and perfect. The loss of these is the loss of an irreplaceable economic resource. Luxury companies understand this, and can help reestablish the value of the manufacturing professions.

In 2007, in an effort to retain the skills of its older workers, BMW launched a pilot program to reengineer certain production lines in Dingolfing, Germany. For example, production platforms feature hoists to spare aging backs, adjustable-height work benches, wooden floors instead of rubber to help hips swivel during repetitive tasks, and instruction screens with a magnifying glass. As a result, BMW discovered that not only were workers able to work safer longer, but productivity went up seven percent, absenteeism fell below the plant's average, and this assembly line's defect rate dropped to zero.[28] Adopting these innovations across their production network allowed BMW to improve the performance of their whole manufacturing system.

The potential to reform manufacturing is constrained by the opposing forces of price and profit. To justify the business case, it is important to develop consumer demand and shareholder support. Here, too, luxury's power to create desirability can play a role. Luxury brand communications have fallen into the pattern of talking about the brand. But first-person brand communications are losing their effectiveness for empowered and informed consumers. The value proposition has to be about the individual's life and their ability to appropriate the brand for their own benefit. Brand communications can be self-centered, but they should be other-focused. The deep relationship between luxury, quality, and longevity can serve as a resource to educate consumers about intelligent spending and drive demand for better goods. Luxury brands can position consumption as a form of investment, which encourages people to buy wisely and value high-quality, long-lasting goods, infusing the product with meaning. This means focusing on the role and value of time as a precious resource in learning, making, and keeping products. This is not just about materials and production methods. It is also about design that can stand the test of time: design that can adapt and last through fashion cycles while remaining interesting and exciting, and thus break our addiction to fast and disposable novelty goods. The investment of time provides functional and financial returns. After all, time is the undercurrent of sustainability. Resisting the pressure of time also allows individuals to make more responsible decisions.

On the shareholder side, this leads to a capitalism that responds to real needs – true value creation – rather than the need to squeeze out every last drop of profit by manipulating demand and creating needs that do not exist in order to justify hyperproduction. This is where true social responsibility comes in. Contrary to Milton Friedman's maxim, the social responsibility of business is not just about maximizing profit, but about maximizing the leadership values of resource stewardship and example setting, generosity, learning, tolerance, and inclusion.

In brief, creating shared value is how luxury brands can seize the opportunity for leadership in a way that is coherent with the ethic of luxury. Luxury can change the value system with its traditionally unusual, counterintuitive business models and out-of-the-box thinking that assigns objective value to the subjective, the unobvious, the intangible. This makes luxury an innovator and agent of change, a leader in the true sense, rather than just a purveyor of pretty things. This can be integrated at whatever level of sustainability or social responsibility the company is prepared to handle. Most importantly, since ultimate luxury and ultimate responsibility are perpetually ahead of us, a company's stakeholders must be made to understand that it is not a fixed goal but a moving target, which fosters innovation and creativity on the road to perfection. Finally, there is no one-size-fits-all approach. Each brand has to look into its own culture, roots, and reasons for existing to find its own unique solution.

Notes

1   www.faberge.com/thebigegghunt.

2   www.faberge.com/news/151-thefabergbigegghunt2014.aspx.

3   www.elephantparadelondon.org.

4   http://auction.thebigegghunt.co.uk.

5   Porter, M.E. and Kramer, M.R. (2011) "Creating shared value: How to reinvent capitalism – and unleash a wave of innovation and growth". *Harvard Business Review*, 89(1/2): 62–77.

6   Pachter, B. (2013) "6 phrases to avoid if you want to be taken seriously at work." *Business Insider*, October 17.

7   Weisberger, L. (2004) *The Devil Wears Prada: A Novel*. Broadway Books.

8   Puma press release (2011) "Puma completes first environmental profit and loss account which values impacts at €145 million." November 16.

9   Kering press release (2012) "PPR introduces environmental and social 5-year targets across luxury and sport & lifestyle brands // PPR acquires stake in wildlife works carbon, REDD carbon offsetting company as part of next phase of sustainability program." April 27.

10   Golbin, P. (ed.) (2009) *Madeleine Vionnet*. Rizzoli.

11   Stock, K. (2013) "Patagonia's 'buy less' plea spurs more buying." *Bloomberg Businessweek*, August 28.

12   Carnegie, A. (2006) *The "Gospel of Wealth" Essays and Other Writings*. Penguin Classics.

13   www.amfar.org/shop/louis-vuitton-cosmetic-case.

14   www.tiffany.com/CSR/.

15   http://uk.loccitane.com/l'occitane's-position-on-animal-testing,83,1,29599, 259188.htm.

16   Hower, M. (2013) "UN report shows significant gap between corporate sustainability intentions and actions." *Sustainable Brands*, September 6.

17   www.pmi.com/eng/tobacco_regulation/pages/tobacco_regulation.aspx.

18   Utting, P. and Zammit, A. (2006) *Beyond Pragmatism: Appraising UN-Business Partnerships*. UNRISD.

19   Lego (2013) *Responsibility Report 2013*. The Lego Group.

20   Lego press release (2013) "First ever official lego model of the UN completed by Ban Ki-Moon." September 20.

21   www.emoya.co.za/p23/accommodation/shanty-town-for-a-unique-accommodation-experience-in-bloemfontein.html.

22   Maslin, N. (2011) "In Haiti, class comes with a peek at lush life." *The New York Times*, May 3.

23   Op. cit., Porter and Kramer.

24   CSV Report of Nestlé Pakistan Limited for the year ended December 31 2012.

25   O'Brien, K. (2012) "How McDonald's came back bigger than ever." *The New York Times Magazine*, May 4.

26   Ibid.

27   Welch, L. (2013) "The way I work: Yvon Chouinard, Patagonia." *Inc.* magazine, March 12.

28   Roth, R. (2010) "How BMW deals with an aging workforce." CBS News, September 5.

6

Creating a culture of shared value

- In order to reconcile the competing needs of business and society, the pursuit of shared value relies on the individual as the common element between the two institutions.

- Brands are composed of people, and so must work to align their values with those of society, define their purpose as citizens, and shape the behavior of their people to suit.

- Luxury brands are not just citizens but leaders, which gives them the ability to raise their stature by influencing the wider community.

There is pressure on companies to do more than make money. Customers still want the best product at the lowest cost. But "best" today means that the product, and thus the brand, must reflect their way of thinking and living, and "cost" today encompasses the holistic costs – psychological, environmental, and so on – of obtaining the product. Employees want more than just a job and a salary. Today's labor force is more attuned to the possibilities for their work to be fulfilling. Company owners want more than just the fastest and highest possible return on their investment.

Shareholders want to know that the company they own is legally compliant, well run, and responsible in managing their business. In addition, indirect stakeholders, such as the people living near a factory or the fans who follow a brand on social media, want more than just a name they recognize and respect. The public now wants to be assured that the company's presence in their lives and communities is a positive influence. These developments show a convergence in the attitudes of all the stakeholders of a brand toward qualitative criteria in addition to quantitative criteria. In an industrial but pre-information economy world, quantity versus quality was a trade-off. Today, people want both.

This is especially true of luxury. Luxury customers want the best of something, they are not willing to accept compromise in terms of design, manufacturing, or functionality. At the same time, luxury customers want the products they want, when they want them, where they want them. This responsiveness is part of what they are paying for. The only exceptions to this rule are when there is a physical constraint. The customer for a one-of-a-kind product, such as bespoke apparel and accessories or a custom-made car or yacht, is obviously willing to allow time for the process. The second exception is when the product, even a standard one, is in such high demand and so desired by customers that they are willing to wait their turn in the production queue. The classic example here is that of the Hermès Birkin bag, the wait for which has grown from a couple of months to more than a year over the past decade.

These two specific situations aside, however, luxury customers are representative of the rest of us. In the preceding chapters, we discussed how there has been an overall increase in prosperity in society and how the fragmentation of institutions and the abstraction of value from material wealth to knowledge is pushing everything to address more than our physical and security needs.

Society as a whole has moved up the levels of Maslow's hierarchy of needs since industrialization and the early 20th-century trials of socioeconomic dislocation and war. The postwar period, dominated by the influence of mass media and globalization, was marked by homogenization and the need to belong. It was only around the turn of this century that technology allowed us to assert ourselves as individuals. So now the focus is on developing our self-esteem and self-actualization. Up until this point, self-esteem was derived from the esteem shown to us by others. It required external validation, and society's propensity toward accepting the lowest common denominator made this more about fitting in with mass opinion rather than challenging it. To stand out required an enormous tolerance for risk and resistance by others. The possibilities for individual expression now open to us via digital technology – social media and so on – allow and even encourage us to challenge the mass approval of others and seek their esteem by standing out from the crowd, showing our uniqueness and originality. This used to be the exclusive domain of artists, but is now accessible to the rest of us. It leads us to self-actualization, the highest level on Maslow's hierarchy, at which individuals pursue their personal feelings of fulfillment.

Businesses must figure out how to integrate this new focus into processes that have, until now, been designed to focus on growth. They must reconcile the competing value demands of different stakeholder groups into one value proposition that is shared among those groups. The challenge for business is how to move from thinking about economic value to shared value, and how to implement value systems, a corporate culture and behavior to turn this ambition into reality.

The shared value model proposed by Michael Porter and Mark Kramer of FSG identifies two spheres; creating business value, defined as investments in long-term competitiveness, and creating social value, defined as investments that address social and environmental objectives.[1] Porter and Kramer locate shared value in the area where these two spheres overlap (Figure 6.1). The definition is a straightforward combination of the two: investments in long-term business competitiveness that simultaneously address social and environmental objectives. On the surface, this is a simple

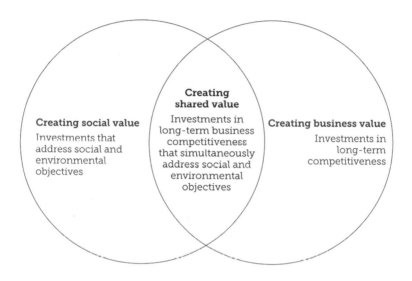

Creating social value

Investments that address social and environmental objectives

Creating shared value

Investments in long-term business competitiveness that simultaneously address social and environmental objectives

Creating business value

Investments in long-term competitiveness

FIGURE 6.1 / FSG model of shared value[1]

repackaging of the three sustainable development pillars – economic, social, and environmental – into something similar to the holistic approach of social responsibility. Bear in mind that, in Chapter 5, we established that social responsibility does not exclude the environment, but integrates it completely into one's broader responsibility to society. Porter and Kramer do take this beyond sustainability or social responsibility. According to them, by focusing on creating shared value, business benefits from serving society. Rather than capturing their share of the economic pie, businesses should seek to make that pie bigger by solving problems that people face and meeting their needs. The opportunities for growth that businesses require come from the exponential growth of the human population, and the consequent explosion of human need, as well as from helping the world manage the increasing complexity of a fragmented, interconnected, and growing modern society.

But this model is of only limited use for luxury brands. Luxury brands may help society address complexity and uncertainty through their relationship with art, as we described in Chapter 4, but luxury does not address needs so much as desires. If anything, it addresses higher level needs, anchored in the metaphysical rather than the physical. At the physical level, the luxury product is not about satisfying a person's basic requirements, but about doing so at a superlative level in a way that connects it with their emotional experience. So, luxury needs a more sophisticated model for creating shared value, which accounts for the individual experience.

The three rings

There is an innate tension between business and society. First, business, by its nature, is competitive, while society must be cooperative. Businesses look to capture market share and attract and keep the best resources at the best conditions for themselves. The success of a community hinges on its ability to share resources and meet the needs of all its members. Second, business thrives on dominance, while society aims for an equitable distribution of opportunities. Businesses look for fluidity, as in unregulated markets, in which they can do whatever they must to jostle for a better position. Society makes rules to promote stability and security, and protect against injustice.

Even with the best of intentions, there will inevitably be tensions between the two. For example, why would a business pay higher wages if the market accepts lower salaries, particularly in times of economic crisis when unemployment is high and company revenues are low? The US debate about raising the minimum wage in the context of high unemployment following the 2008 crisis was not just about raising the minimum level of pay, but about whether that level provides a living wage to workers. Its opponents on the business side argue that keeping the minimum wage low would encourage businesses to hire more workers and allow them to keep prices low for struggling consumers. Its proponents on the social side, meanwhile, argue that employment that does not provide workers with sufficient means for subsistence is a false benefit that only serves to exacerbate economic inequality and keeps consumers struggling. It has become accepted that in order to make money, business must be selfish, merciless, even unscrupulous. It is only after having accumulated wealth that a business can afford to indulge more socially minded impulses by engaging in philanthropic acts that support charitable works and do good for society as a whole.

But what does it really mean when we say that "business does this" or "society wants that"? The *World English Dictionary* defines a company as "a business enterprise" and "a number of people gathered together." So, the firm is not one monolithic entity, but is assembled from a group of people joined in the pursuit of its mission. The action of a company is then the sum of the actions of all the individuals, from the decisions made by management to the activities undertaken by labor to implement those decisions. Those activities are also the product of the decisions made by individuals about whether and how to execute the work requested by their bosses. The individual is absolved of personal responsibility for the consequences of their actions outside the firm (within the limits of legal compliance), because these consequences result from the cumulative action of the company. Similarly, the *World English Dictionary* defines society as "a system of human organizations" and "an organized group of people associated for some specific purpose."

So neither is society one monolithic entity, but is assembled from a group of people joined for their shared benefit. The parallel between the two is even more obvious in French, where *une société* can refer either to a society or a company and *la société* can refer either to a specific firm or society in general.

The common, constituent part of businesses and firms is the individual. The difference is in their reason for coming together. The tension arises when these reasons diverge, forcing the individual to choose between them and act in one sphere in a way that is counterproductive to the other. Having to exist simultaneously in both spheres pushes individuals into conflict with themselves. This becomes exacerbated when individuals choose to commit their loyalties entirely to one sphere or another, which pushes people into conflict with each other. This leads, at best, to the competing requirements of different stakeholders, which companies have to balance. At worst, it spills over into society, causing polarization, class conflict, political gridlock, even civil war.

Not accounting for the individual dimension is where Porter and Kramer's model falls short. It misses our need to fit within the values of our social groups as well as the need to fit within the values of the corporate culture for which we work. This gives us our sense of belonging and furthers our self-esteem by allowing us to rise in social standing and move up the corporate structure. But people can behave one way in their personal lives and a completely different, sometimes antagonistic way in their professional lives. This is at the heart of the challenge of social responsibility. As citizens, we may complain about businesses polluting the environment, avoiding taxes, or corrupting the political process. We may debate with friends about how money and marketing are driving us toward an ever more meaningless, materialist culture. We may worry that our children spend too much time obsessing over celebrities and fashion trends. But when we go to work, we often check those values at the door. We look for ways to help our companies cut costs by finding shortcuts and loopholes, and by influencing governments to loosen regulations that can stifle the company's profit margins. We look for ways to help our companies grow revenues by coming up with new and more tempting product offers and marketing campaigns. We look for ways to engage consumers by playing into the popular culture and getting the media to cover an accelerating cycle of "must haves." Then, as consumers, we reward ourselves for our hard work by buying things that give us pleasure before going home and worrying about how society is going down the drain.

Brenda Romero is a game designer famous for the successful Wizardry video games franchise. In 2009, she developed a board game called *Train*, which was not meant to be commercialized, but which caused a stir in the games industry because of its ability to make players confront the difficult emotion of taking responsibility for their actions. Players follow instructions to efficiently load little yellow pegs, representing people, onto trains. The winner is the one who gets the most people to their destination. Good, right? The challenge is in intentionally designed procedural gaps, which oblige the players to agree on the rules going forward. The twist comes when the destination is revealed to be Auschwitz, with the consequent realization that the players have been competing to send a maximum number of people to their deaths. According to Dean Takahashi: "The key emotion that Romero said she wanted the player to feel was 'complicity'."[2] This complicity comes from blithely following instructions and even contributing to them by coming to a consensus with other players about how to fill the procedural gaps. Once acknowledged, this sense of complicity causes people to react with shame and even try and subvert the game, as by hiding pegs.

Train demonstrates how easily individuals can and do subordinate their own values to the larger value system imposed by the context – be it by their community or their work, how easily people are "trained" – particularly when the full consequences of their actions are unclear. The difference between real life and a game is that once the player understands the point of the game, they can opt out. Things are not so simple in real life. Leaving the "game" has financial, personal, and professional costs. Few people can easily walk away from a job when they have obligations to their family and creditors, and aspirations for their own careers. Even as consumers, even as citizens, people look away from inconvenient truths. They may choose to willfully not know the consequences of their actions because their obligations within the rules are enough of a burden. Even if companies can form a consensus among their people to change the system, it is still difficult to abandon existing practices – difficult and often pointless. In real life, if a "player" leaves the "game," this does not mean that the game ends. Until the whole of society has agreed that the goal of the game is inconsistent with the goals of society, and implements the political and legal reforms to change the game, walking away from the table only frees a seat for another player. So, boycotting the game only serves one's own sense of integrity. In the bigger picture, it accomplishes nothing until enough individuals opt out so that their seats are left vacant and the game ceases to exist.

We rarely openly articulate our deepest values and ideals in daily life, but they are visible through our actions. However, it can happen that we feel obliged to act in ways that differ from what we hold in our hearts. To be in harmony with oneself, there must be conformity between one's values and how they actually live. But the truth is that we often live in a state of personal–professional conflict because we have not determined which values are responsible for our choices, and our actions and choices do not stem from our most firmly held beliefs. Only at a turning point of crisis do we stop to reassess. This is why people will often change career paths after a life-changing event or a near-death experience, such as an accident or a serious illness, or a strong emotional experience such as the loss of a job or a loved one, or even in response to external events such as a natural disaster or a catastrophe like 9/11. These existential moments cause us to reflect on our lives up until that point and they confront us with the combination of our deepest values and our current priorities and behaviors. It does not have to be that traumatic. The roots of the word "crisis" come from the Greek *krísi*, which connotes decision or judgment. So, any turning point will do. The almost universal experience of the midlife crisis comes when people have reached a point in their lives, often their careers, where they get a sense of the time they have left to live and ask themselves how they want to spend it and the legacy they want to leave. According to Sylvie Bénard, environment director at LVMH:

> I often get approached by people looking to change jobs. They have reached a certain level of career success, but having achieved that, they realize that they also want to do good. I tell them to stay where they are. The environment needs allies throughout an organization, and I tell them that they can do even more good by changing things in their current role.

So, we can bring our actions in line with our values without abandoning the game, but by changing how it is played. Classical Greek philosopher Socrates advised: "it is the greatest good for a man to discuss virtue every day." Socrates was one of the earliest in a long line of thinkers who believed that the more dialogue we create around our deepest values and ideals, the more we reinforce them, and the more likely we are to act accordingly. Even if – perhaps, especially because – the dialogue leaves people with a keener awareness of how much more we do not know than we do know about our values and our willingness and ability to enact them. Research shows that critical self-examination of values affects subsequent behavior. In psychological studies, subjects were asked to participate in an activity that measured how much they discriminated against a randomly created group of people in the lab. One group first spent ten minutes expressing and defending their attitude towards equality. A second group was simply reminded of the value of equality but not asked to defend their views. In the subsequent activity, the first group demonstrated less discrimination than the second.[3] Those subjects who articulated their values were more likely to apply those values to their behavior, supporting Socrates' use of critical self-examination as a bridge between values and action.

Recognizing the role of individual values in collective outcomes, the shared value model in this book has three spheres: business, social, and individual. Taking Porter and Kramer's definitions as a starting point, our definition for the individual sphere can be seen as: investments that encourage leadership and build relationships between individual stakeholders that help align social and business interests. This opens up critical self-examination within people to reconcile their conflicting personal and professional expectations. It also opens up dialogue between individuals, based on this reconciliation, which makes consensus with others and solution seeking possible. Rather than pitting stakeholder interests against one another, it opens up channels for mutual understanding, aligning objectives, and sharing the ideas and resources necessary to change the game. By being the common element of each, the individual binds the molecules of business and society together.

We then take it a step further, by removing the associations imposed by the word "investment" and focusing directly on the value delivered in each sphere. This shifts the emphasis from the costs to the benefits. While focusing on the costs keeps people thinking in a mindset of less, focusing on the benefits opens up the possibility of more. This is also how luxury approaches product value. From this, individual value means providing opportunities for self-actualization, accomplishment, and validation. These connect to the business values of product offerings for consumers, meaningful work for employees, and profits for investors. They connect to social value by providing responsibility and leadership that lead to community enhancement.

These create the dynamics that make three-dimensional shared value possible. Porter and Kramer's approach is strengthened by the addition of two new overlaps. By linking the individual and social spheres, we unleash the dynamic of humanity and solidarity; the compassion and cooperation that are at the root of what differentiates humans from animals in being able to form a society and build civilization. By linking the individual and business spheres, we formalize relationships and objective setting to create a dynamic of consensus and commitment. At the core, we find three-dimensional shared value, which engages the individual to solve business and social problems. The original shared value model is now expanded from sustainability to include engagement, through the ability to align objectives and share resources, and establishes companies as citizens of the community (Figure 6.2).

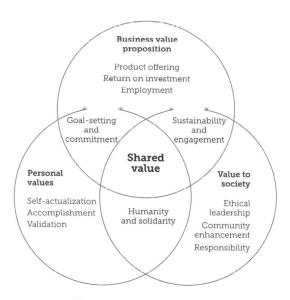

FIGURE 6.2 Three-dimensional model of shared value

The "give" model

The question, then, is how to reconcile the vast diversity of individual perspectives and point them all in the same direction to achieve a goal. Financial incentives are no longer enough as people are waking up to qualitative motivations. Meaning comes from having a sense of purpose, that one's actions have impact and change something. More and more, this is becoming aligned with creating harmony rather than just filling personal coffers. So, the shared value that companies provide is about helping individuals achieve their qualitative goals. Their purpose is bound up in what it is about the world they want to change. This is especially true of luxury, which addresses higher level needs of belonging, esteem, and self-actualization. Luxury is not in the security business, and so it is freed from defending the status quo. Like artists, and other creators of shared value, luxury firms have a strong vision of an ideal world, one that is essential to creating the appetite for luxury. Once they themselves are in harmony with that vision, they can go about changing the game. This means that they have to realign the relationships between individuals through which the brand functions, both internally and externally – the brand's owners, its employees, its customers, and the broader community.

Today, the brand's relationship with its stakeholders functions according to a "take" model (Figure 6.3). This is not an impeachment of the company as greedy, taking from its stakeholders. On the contrary, the company has to be greedy because it is constantly being bled of resources. In this system, not just the company but all the actors are perpetually "on the take." This is because the "take" model is based on transactional exchanges rather than relationships. The brand exchanges money and benefits for the labor of employees. It exchanges products for customers' money. It exchanges marketing investment for the expectations of the community, which is converted into customer demand. All this is in order to exchange profits for the continued support of investors. In a transactional view of work, the parties meet to take from one another. Money and utility, the providers of which are easily substituted, are the basis of this model. As a result, a company's resources are taxed in multiple ways just to feed a single stream of returns.

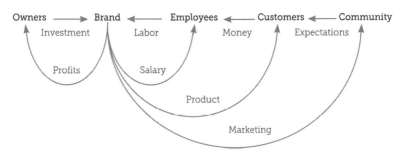

FIGURE 6.3 The "take" model of stakeholder relationships

Businesses may think the "take" model works in their favor because it is transactional and their investment is measurable against the returns they gain. For example, how many hours of work or how much output they can expect in return for the salary paid to employees, or how many products will sell at a particular price. The "take" model works on the assumption that each of the exchanges is hermetically sealed, and that the value chain from a company's owners through their employees to their customers and community is a simple linear construct. But, in a transactional relationship, each party gets only what they pay for and will therefore give only as much as they feel is justified by the price. When they feel they can get a better deal elsewhere, they will move.

To use a concept articulated by James Moore, companies exist in a business ecosystem where they are in simultaneous competition and cooperation with other players.[4] Like animals in the wild, they both need each other but compete for the same resources.

A lion predator needs his antelope prey, but he must share the watering hole with the antelope if he is to be nourished by its meat. Alternately, the antelope needs his herd for the safety it provides, but competes with his own cohort to graze. When one species disappears from an ecosystem, it can take a range of other species with it, but at the same time, it creates opportunities for other species, which may have been marginal to the ecosystem, to suddenly flourish and become dominant. However, a company is not just an actor in the larger business ecosystem, it is also an ecosystem itself, one with porous inner and outer boundaries. Thanks to technology and rapidly evolving attitudes to the work–life divide, individuals are no longer confined to just one role in the organization. Increasingly, an employee can simultaneously be a client, an observer, or a shareholder, or any combination of these roles. So, the organization is part of an ecosystem where the different players are linked, internally and externally, not in a linear or one-to-one relationship but in a complex web of multifaceted relationships. Twitch one strand of this web and it sets several, perhaps all the strands vibrating, creating a resonance across the entire system.

FIGURE 6.4 The "give" model of stakeholder relationships

In the "give" model, every actor gets back more than they pay for (Figure 6.4). The company gives their employees not just a job, but a purpose. The sense of meaning generated by having a purpose rather than just a set of tasks and responsibilities contributes to employee motivation and increases their productivity, which they give back to the organization. Employees, who are the interface of the brand with the customer, now carry out more than the simple sales transaction of products for money. They provide solutions rooted in the company's purpose, recognizing that customers are not just consumers looking for products, but part of a much bigger community where complex issues and decisions intersect with their consumer behavior. The move from products to solutions validates the consumer as a whole person. People naturally reward validation with loyalty. This is a heartfelt and more intimate kind of loyalty, which goes beyond the loyalty created by engagement programs such as preferred customer discounts, private sales, frequent flyer miles, and social media campaigns designed to keep customers consuming. These programs are just another form of transaction. What is important, however, is the intent and substance of the relationship. By providing people with solutions that go above and beyond the product, the brand is making a contribution to the community. This raises the brand's standing by increasing the amount of goodwill felt toward the brand by the larger public. This is the key ingredient of brand love and reputation, and increases the brand's value as an asset. As a result of the benefits the brand gets from the leadership of its owners, who direct it toward a purpose, the brand provides not only financial returns, but also prestige, with the trust and standing to exert even more leadership.

The "take" model drains the company of various resources in order to return revenues, keeping the company focused on marginal benefits and cost mitigation. It is powered by thinking small, which results in a race to the bottom. On the other hand, the "give" model creates a virtuous cycle in the behavior of the company by reinforcing their output of purpose with multiple streams of support, allowing the company to reinvest these in continuing their work. It aims for bigger. It is a race to the top. The "give" model does not replace the "take" model but adds another, metaphysical dimension to it, giving us the combined model, shown in Figure 6.5. The relationships inherent in a shared value model do not replace the transactions, but augment them by giving meaning to the whole process. This contributes to individuals' sense of fulfillment. Stakeholders are no longer beholden to one another in the moment. The brand no longer has to buy their loyalty. Instead, they voluntarily and continually give back to it in the form of the strength of its position in the community, the trust it enjoys, and its consequent influence. Self-interest still drives this approach, but seeks to increase the total amount of value in the system. And by contributing, it also recognizes that individual interests thrive best when the whole environment thrives. The purpose is based in a contribution to the community.

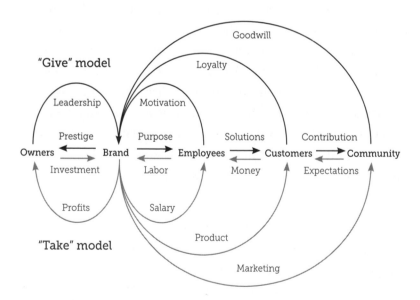

FIGURE 6.5 / The "give" and "take" models together

Look at the example of Apple. Contrary to popular belief, Apple are not an inventor. Personal computers existed long before Apple came on the scene. Even smartphones, for which Apple are now particularly celebrated, were first developed more than a decade before the iPhone, by Ericsson, BlackBerry and others, combining the functionalities of mobile phones and other consumer electronics, such as digital organizers, home computers, cameras, and so on. Apple's purpose is not even to be a technological innovator. Rather, their innovation is driven by the aim of humanizing the technological experience. Apple realized this vision through "skeuomorphism," where the user interface emulates objects in real life. On a computer "desktop," for example, you move around and layer documents the way you would do with papers on a desk. This was first conceived of by Apple before flowing back into Microsoft's and other companies' products. An Apple product is designed to be intuitive. Switch it on and start to use it. The product does not even come with a user guide. By humanizing the use of technology, Apple have built an almost evangelical loyalty to the brand. This is not just among the customers who spend days in line for a new release. Apple are not known for paying particularly high salaries to their retail staff. But the personnel at Apple stores are proactively helpful and highly informed because they are driven by a passion that is converted into caring for the customer. This is a manifestation of the same sense of purpose shared right up the Apple value chain, from the programmers who develop the software, the designers of the hardware, to the standards pursued by managers. The sense of purpose has resulted in Apple's commercial success and the stratospheric rise in their share price. That is not to say that Apple are a gentle saint. Steve Jobs was notoriously difficult to work with. The company have been criticized for working with manufacturers in China that employ abusive labor practices. Their environmental track record needs work. Their community of followers now pushes them in those areas as well.

The specific nature of a particular company's purpose depends on its own story. Not every company is in the business of technological innovation. A brand derives its purpose from its backstory of values and origin, the founding spark that motivated an entrepreneur to change something in the world. This is ultimately the road to citizenship. It uses the company's competitive nature to further the cooperation needs of a society. Across all examples of corporate purpose, the common ingredient is the human dimension, which in one way or another is about caring for other people. Gary Vaynerchuk, author of the *The Thank You Economy*, says that:

> especially in the luxury category ... we are living through the humanization of business ... We have now conditioned ourselves as humans to actually have relationships with logos ... Now it's going to come down to: Does business have the ability to be human? Do we strategize for sales or do we actually give a fuck?[5]

A tremendous body of knowledge is emerging on corporate purpose. Edelman, the world's largest independent PR firm, published their Goodpurpose study in 2012.[6] The research found that 87 percent of consumers believe that business should place at least equal weight on societal and business issues, but only 28 percent of consumers believe that business is performing well in this regard. It also found that consumers are more willing to name and publicly shame companies they feel do not live up to their social obligations. Beyond communications, consumers say they will avoid buying a company's products and even refuse to invest in it if they do not feel that the company contributes to a good cause. (In practice, companies have found this to be not quite so clear-cut: actual consumer behavior has yet to fully reflect the survey responses.) Consumers' expectations for a company's contribution take a familiar form: philanthropy and process or partner innovation. But the stakes here are rising as well, with consumers increasingly asking companies to provide educational information and dialogue opportunities, and to work with government, with the burden being on CEOs to proactively address societal issues.

Adam Grant, management professor at the University of Pennsylvania's Wharton School, identified three types of corporate culture: takers, givers, and matchers. [7] Taker cultures have high levels of internal competition, which cause colleagues to withhold assistance and information from one another, and undermine each other's work in order to get ahead individually. In matcher cultures, the category into which most organizations fall, colleagues help one another, but in quid pro quo exchanges of traded favors that occur within closed loops of relationships that do not include outsiders. In giver cultures, colleagues help one another without expecting anything in return, by sharing information, mentoring, and making connections. While they have to contend with issues such as distraction and inefficiency, giver cultures achieve the highest levels of performance. Grant found that:

> the frequency with which employees help one another predicts sales revenues in pharmaceutical units and retail stores; profits, costs, and customer service in banks; creativity in consulting and engineering firms; productivity in paper mills; and revenues, operating efficiency, customer satisfaction, and performance quality in restaurants.

He cites research by the University of Washington, which found that competitive teams finished tasks more quickly than cooperative teams, but did so at lower levels of accuracy because members would not share crucial information with one another. Furthermore, the study found that teams that were incentivized to transition from competition to cooperation had trouble doing so. People had lost trust in colleagues who had previously been seen as competitors. Speed decreased, but quality did not improve.

This is clear evidence that the collaborative culture of communities – with aspects such as sharing, trust, and even altruism – transposed to companies through the "give" model can deliver measurable performance benefits beyond those offered by traditional competitive approaches. So, the returns on investing in being a good corporate citizen are not only a matter of faith. Furthermore, it creates fertile ground for cultivating leadership within and by the company, which generates prestige in return for the leader's contribution to individual as well as collective wellbeing. It is a much stronger leadership status, given by the support of the constituency rather than taken in the pursuit of power.

Connecting the brand to the individual

Passionate support for a brand cannot be demanded. A company must inspire it. Once a company has aligned their business, social, and individual value propositions, and identified their purpose, the question is: How can the company orient their stakeholders to support this purpose? The answer is to empower individuals to also align their values across the three spheres in order to exercise their autonomy of judgment. This kind of individual empowerment can and usually is seen as dangerous by organizations because they feel it gives them less control. Most brands are protective of themselves and closely control internal and external information and decision-making processes. Luxury brands can be particularly ferocious about this control because so much of their cachet is bound up in the brand's mystique. But the transparency inherent in combining the business, social, and personal dimensions builds trust internally and externally. The rules that determine the level of personal autonomy are dictated by a company's corporate governance structures, so what are these structures responding to? In Chapter 5, we talked about the importance of intent in organizing processes. Does a company move from undirected corporate governance, or is the corporate governance meant to support their shared value creation? In a similar way, are companies encouraging their people to follow rules or fulfill their purpose?

LRN are a consultancy that inspire companies to "principled performance" and help them build resilient and innovative cultures. LRN's work identifies three types of corporate culture: blind obedience, informed acquiescence, or self-governance.[8] Blind obedience organizations, like military organizations, show strong top-down leadership, and even coercion through rules and policing. Informed acquiescence organizations, like religion, rely on performance-based rewards and punishments to motivate people to follow the rules, policies, and procedures established by what they believe to be a skilled management team. Self-governance organizations, like artists, are primarily values based, where purpose informs decision making and guides all employee and company behavior. These cultures have consequences in determining the company's ability to balance long- and short-term thinking. While obedience and acquiescence cultures place importance on the immediate benefits of following rules, self-governance encourages all employees to be leaders with a focus on long-term legacy. This gives their work meaning, which contributes to their sense of fulfillment. But where artists can function entirely on raw values, organizations need to get people to function together.

Dov Seidman is the founder of LRN and the author of *How: Why HOW We Do Anything Means Everything*. His work with the Boston Research Group found that employee engagement was falling across the board. A 2011 study by the Boston Research Group found that 27 percent of corporate bosses and only 4 percent of employees believe their firms are inspiring places to work.[9] The lower figure is perhaps less surprising, because if those responsible for a firm's governance do not find it meaningful, how can those who work for them care about it at all? He calls current employee engagement cultures "out to lunch" – literally, companies feel they can improve their employee relationships with a proliferation of social events and team-building exercises. In truth, these often backfire by encroaching on an employee's personal life and their productivity. What is missing is the trust that allows organizations to empower their people. LRN's 2012 *The How Report* found that there is a large gap in perceptions of self-governance between bosses and employees.[10] Senior management consistently felt that their organizations encourage more self-governance and less coercion than the overall employee population. To some extent, this is natural, as senior managers' responsibilities involve them in more lateral thinking and strategic decisions, which innately imbue their roles with more creativity than those charged with implementation. But this also concentrates a feeling of autonomy at the top, which does not disseminate trust throughout the organization, thus undermining the reciprocal engagement that leads to a sense of meaning and fulfillment for employees.

According to LRN's research findings, derived from observations of 36,000 employees in 18 countries:

> employees who experience a high-trust environment are 22 times more likely to be willing to take risks that could benefit the company. Employees functioning in an organization of high trust are eight times more likely to report higher levels of innovation relative to their competition. And finally, employees functioning in a culture of high trust, risk-taking, and innovation are six times more likely to report elevated levels of financial performance compared to the competition.

To build trust, companies need to extend the sense of ownership that senior managers feel to all levels of the organization. Only then will the corporate culture and the benefits of its purpose flow out into the community. If you are going to instill employees with a sense of purpose, they also need the liberty to pursue that purpose according to their own methods. Otherwise, it is not a purpose, it is an obligation.

To allow workers to serve a purpose, they need the autonomy to express their values through their company's actions in a way that is coherent with the company's values. Thus, a company should not police their actions, but build a culture where they know what is expected of them and can act according to their values, because a certain core set is aligned with the company's. Also, since actions can transform value, there is a pedagogical role for the company in transforming the person, liberating them from blindly following instructions to the legal minimum.

The brand can be a tool for building a culture of self-governance. Individuals share an essential structure of needs based on our biological origins and the evolution of the human psyche. Abraham Maslow's "theory of human motivation" presents these in a concise and useful form, which is a familiar business tool.[11] Viewed from above, Maslow's hierarchy of needs can be seen as a set of concentric circles, providing an opportunity to establish parallels between the layers of human needs and the common elements of a brand platform. Translating the brand to the individual experience shows how it can be the basis for need fulfillment on many levels (Figure 6.6). Businesses are often conceived in terms of their utilitarian actions: the manifestation of their value proposition to customers. More sophisticated models seek to frame these first in terms of an overarching mission, with vision and values making the transition to the execution of actual work. Shared value is partly an emotional intelligence appeal, and luxury brands operate at the emotional and business nexus. A brand platform centered on the individual puts values at the core. Defining the self first gives meaning and direction to all the other elements as a source of motivation.

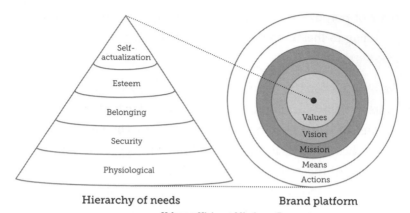

Hierarchy of needs   Brand platform

Values + Vision + Mission = Purpose

FIGURE 6.6 Connecting the brand to the individual

In the same way that a company can either move from compliance to shared value, or use their pursuit of shared value to raise the level of their actions beyond compliance, so a company can either let their actions determine their mission, vision, and values, or use their values to inform their vision, formulate their mission in service to that vision, and align their actions to suit. This parallels how people can either move up Maslow's hierarchy, pursuing higher level needs only once their physical and security needs are met, or use their need for self-actualization to meet their lower level needs by achieving success. The vast majority of people work to move up Maslow's hierarchy. The fear of not meeting their basic and security needs keeps them from taking the risks that lead to self-actualization. But a special category of people, those driven by belief and purpose – artists like Vincent van Gogh and Leonardo da Vinci, or social activists like Nelson Mandela and Mahatma Gandhi – actually prioritize their need for fulfillment over their needs for security, money, and even sex. Luxury brands function like artists. They are not in the business of creating just any product to sell and make profit. They are capable of sacrificing boundless growth in order to stay true to their vision. They are in the business of ennobling the human experience. This obviously happens at the physical and emotional levels, but they can influence the purpose-driven level as well.

When PPR changed their name to Kering in 2013, it was intended to signal a new strategy for the company. Under the leadership of François-Henri Pinault, Kering were evolving from a diversified holding company into an apparel and accessories group focused on luxury and the sport and lifestyle sector. In addition, Kering were making sustainability a core pillar of their corporate strategy. The name Kering resounds with the pronunciation of "caring" and takes its root from "ker," which means "home" in Breton, Brittany being the native region of the Pinault family. The new name also traces its roots to *Home*, the nature documentary made by photographer Yann Arthus-Bertrand, the production of which had been supported by PPR. The original name of PPR's sustainability department was PPR Home, showing how the company's commitment to sustainability came to define their corporate identity. In implementing this commitment, Kering rely on an operational style called "freedom within a framework," by which their brands and their people are empowered to find their own ways to accomplish the group's goals in accordance with the group's values. Kering states their mission as allowing their customers to express, fulfill, and enjoy themselves through their products. This is all summed up in the Kering signature statement: "Empowering Imagination," which we conclude to be their purpose. Empowering the imagination of people within and outside the organization is the contribution that fuels their mission.

If companies do not manage their corporate culture, a culture will emerge anyway, like weeds in a garden. Rather than policing their employees' behavior, companies must establish a culture where the rules of behavior are not just explicitly written out, but where the expectations for what is appropriate are implicitly understood by all.

One ring to rule them all

Luxury as the marriage between art and business means that it does not have to choose between working up or down Maslow's hierarchy, but can reconcile the two. What differentiates the starving artist from the successful artist, and the angry street protester from the leader of social change is their ability to merge their values with those of the market and community. Luxury firms have already mastered many of the challenges facing other companies, such as providing personally attentive customer service, superior working conditions, creative freedom, respect for raw materials, and are good at engaging social causes, such as women's rights, biodiversity, cultural preservation, and education. But in an ever more competitive world, do they give up this lead to competitive pressure or can they exert outward influence so that the values that make luxury a leader can be shared more broadly throughout the business and social cultures? Many nonluxury companies have picked up on the verbal and visual vocabulary of luxury. So, luxury does have an influence. How can it be more than stylistic and actually contribute to the creation of shared value? If luxury spreads its culture throughout business and society, will it not surrender the very thing that sets it apart?

No. Because luxury's advantage is not just its ideals, it is also the execution of luxury, and not every company is able or even willing to invest the time and talent needed for the dazzling level of artistry and quality that define luxury. And not every customer is able or even willing to appreciate them. Even in an ideal world, there will always be a lag. So, because luxury's culture will spread from luxury, it will always belong to luxury. Furthermore, as the culture spreads, it will push luxury ahead to open up perspectives that have not yet been experienced. That is, after all, how luxury remains luxurious.

Monet's *Water Lilies* is one of the most familiar images in art. Countless reproductions of the iconic work hang as posters in doctors' waiting rooms, adorn desks as calendars, liven up sofas as throw pillows, and protect people from the weather as scarves and umbrellas. This has not diminished the number of people wanting to see the original work. In fact, the painting's fame has increased the number of people wanting to come to Paris precisely to see the massive original adorning the curved walls of the Musée de l'Orangerie for themselves and to Giverny to see the real gardens that inspired Monet and the universe within which he lived and worked. Of course, the *Water Lilies* is one of a kind. Forget about aspiring to one day be rich enough to afford the painting. You cannot even aspire to own it. Everyone knows that the version you have is an imitation. But the imitation has only driven the appetite for the real thing.

Luxury goods are different from the *Water Lilies*. They exist in multiple examples. We can aspire to own them, so it is easier to pass an imitation off as the real thing. This makes them vulnerable to the effect of forgeries, the bête noire of the most popular luxury brands. But this popularity has also caused the legitimate stylistic imitation that has been hailed as the democratization of design. It has raised the bar for consumer tastes by opening our eyes to the possibilities luxury has discovered. In the same way that the Impressionists broke barriers about the way artists represent the world, luxury breaks barriers about the way we experience an object through the senses and through the emotions the product can evoke. The posters and umbrellas are pretty, but they have nowhere near the impact and emotional satisfaction of the original work of art. So, luxury can drive the appetite for the real thing, even in a world where imitations are widely available. By increasing the appeal of luxury and heightening our appreciation for what luxury really represents, luxury can drive consumers to desire better things. They may not all be able to afford "luxury" goods, but they can be pushed to look for products that are authentically better rather than for a proliferation of cheap imposters. When you increase the understanding and appreciation for the real thing, you are also increasing the pool of potential luxury customers.

This brings us back to the dialogue that luxury has with individuals, paralleling the dialogue that art has with individuals, as we discussed in Chapter 4. For this dialogue to work, it is crucial to get past the urge to market. Just chatting with fans on social media is not enough. The quality of that conversation is defined by its substance, and the substance is defined by the character of the interlocutors. A self-absorbed person at a dinner party will have an equally vapid Facebook page, likely an endless stream of duck-faced selfies; whereas an interesting, intelligent person is likely to use Facebook to share their insights and observations about the world, articles and interesting ideas from others, as well as support causes and call attention to important issues. They enlarge your horizon by being a window onto the wider world. When brands see social media in particular, and their stakeholder engagement more generally, as a platform for self-aggrandizement, they effectively become a billboard that demands our attention but obstructs our view. We may look at it for a bit, but the instinct is to get past it and see the world beyond.

Our values determine our behaviors, but the reverse is also true: by acting in a certain way, we mold our thoughts to our actions, and gradually adapt our values to our behaviors. This is the key to enculturation, which may happen unconsciously, as in parenting or peer pressure in schools, or consciously, as in religious education or indoctrination.[12] Because companies exist in ecosystems, they are subject to coevolution. They influence their environment to evolve, and evolve in response to environmental influences. Just as organizations coevolve in their ecosystems along with their suppliers and competitors, employees internally coevolve with the company they work for and also have an impact on how the company evolves. Thus, the employee is a real connection between the inside and outside worlds of the company. Today, more than ever, with a single individual coexisting in multiple stakeholder categories, companies are less hermetically sealed entities than they are porous vehicles. This dynamic can put the company either in harmony or in dissonance with the objectives of society. By creating a culture that causes people to act in a particular way, they can have a viral impact on the community. They can also learn from their environment by listening to the behaviors and expectations their own people bring in from outside.

The overarching debate about the role of companies in society boils down to corporate citizenship. If a corporation is legally considered to be a person, it is subject to the same responsibilities as all other members of society and is to be judged based on its contribution and moral character. So, the behavior of a brand cannot be separated from the behavior of the individuals that comprise that brand. Luxury is exemplary. This makes it more than a citizen. It makes a luxury brand a leader. By establishing the brand as a culture that drives individual behavior, a company can spread its leadership culture to the entire community. By basing its culture on a purpose that improves the ecosystem, a company can raise its stature and enhance its ability to lead. By using the values widely shared by individuals, it can align its values as a business with the values held by society.

Notes

1 Porter, M. and Kramer, M. (2011) "Creating shared value: How to reinvent capitalism – and unleash a wave of innovation and growth". *Harvard Business Review*, 89(1/2): 62–77.

2 Takahashi, D. (2013) "Brenda Romero's *Train* board game will make you ponder." *Gamesbeat*, May 11.

3 Maio, G. (2010) *Psychology of Human Values*. Psychology Press.

4   Moore, J. (1993) "Predators and prey: A new ecology of competition." *Harvard Business Review*, 71(3): 75–86.

5   Vaynerchuk, G. (2011) *The Thank You Economy: How Business Must Adapt to Social Media*. HarperBusiness. Also watch the video at www. youtube.com/watch?v=2UkiM3OaHxw.

6   Edelman (2012) *Goodpurpose 2012: Global Consumer Survey*.

7   Grant, A. (2013) "Givers take all: The hidden dimension of corporate culture." *McKinsey Quarterly*, April.

8   LRN (2012) *The How Report: New Metrics for a New Reality: Rethinking the Source of Resiliency, Innovation, and Growth*. LRN Corporation.

9   Seidman, D. (2012) "(Almost) everything we think about employee engagement is wrong." *Forbes*, September 20.

10   Op cit., LRN.

11   Maslow, A. (2013) *A Theory of Human Motivation*. Martino Fine Books.

12   Kottak, C. (2011) *Window on Humanity: A Concise Introduction to Anthropology*, 5th edn. McGraw-Hill.

Adapting the business model

---

* Humanity does not have a business case. If companies are going to adapt to the expectations of their stakeholders, they need to get from a business case to a value case.

* Value respects the individual over the system.

* Luxury and innovation only demonstrate their business case after the fact. Being focused on value and individual experience, luxury is perfectly positioned to serve as a value model for other types of business.

The evidence supporting a move to a business model designed around the human experience is overwhelming. Thought leadership work on the culture, functioning, and reputation of organizations by consultancies such as McKinsey, FSG, Edelman, and Burson-Marsteller all points to the same conclusion: companies improve their performance by aligning their processes to people and not the other way around. This is supported by academic research at universities like Harvard and Stanford, which looks at business as a tool for social innovation. Consumer surveys by the Pew Research Center and Gallup confirm these attitudes at the popular level.

Beyond the numbers, it is also intuitive. Reflect on your own life experience, ambitions, and desires. Talk to your friends and see which attitudes toward work, consumption, and money drive people and underlie the achievements of highly respected individuals. Notice the difference in happiness levels between those who work to live and those who live to work. The classic example of people driven by "the system" is their desire to milk it and get out. Finally, look at the lessons of history. We described how the whole of human history has been a movement toward the validation of the individual. In this light, being on the right side of history is a simple matter of pattern recognition.

So why is it proving to be such a struggle? The human resources manager at one luxury goods firm told us that the level of internal competition is so high they sometimes forget that their real competition is outside the group. The executive in charge of finding talent for another major luxury brand told us, matter of factly: "We don't spend a lot of time on employees' sense of fulfillment. That is their own responsibility. In any case, they line up outside the door to work for us." The problem lies in the business case. As the director for sustainable development at one major brand told us, her company functions on quarterly results and any initiative must be justifiable by those metrics.

In the American South before the Civil War, there was a business case for slavery. When plantations failed after emancipation because they could not be run profitably with paid labor, it revealed the shaky foundations of the entire regional economy. While the North had industrialized, the South held firmly to its old ways of doing things. Not only did the South's business case perpetuate the greatest of all evils, it allowed its defenders to ignore the structural rot that was occurring all around them. By looking at only narrow and immediate benefits, the South's complacency killed the need for innovation. The North, by embracing technological progress and Enlightenment ideals, kept itself moving forward.

We raise this example because, in trying to bring business toward a more responsible model, we are often confronted with demands for a business case. How will this increase sales? How will this increase our margins? How will this increase productivity? How will this lower costs? When a company wants to improve their environmental footprint or their social practices, but are tangled up in these sorts of questions, we have to call out their intentions as disingenuous. There is no doubt that a company's profitability is essential to its survival. But conducting responsible, sustainable business is not about sacrificing profitability. It is about using the human dimension to drive innovation forward. Without this, a company will wake up to find itself with its back against the wall, where the only option is abject surrender. It must not let the business case be a ball and chain, preventing the organization from moving forward because it is tethered to old ways of thinking.

While shared value is linked to the concept of social responsibility, in truth, it is a return to the value creation at the heart of private enterprise. Create something that the market values, price it appropriately, and be rewarded for your endeavor. What has changed over time is the definition of value. The original value of a product was in its utility. With the financialization of the entire economy that occurred after World War II, that value shifted to a product's profit potential. This was the point at which shareholders replaced consumers as the real customers of a company. But now, the definitions of both "customer" and "value" are on the move again. With the world more interconnected and companies more transparent, the customer is now a complex web of stakeholders with a variety of often competing demands and expectations. From a value standpoint, this boils down to the role of the company in society generally.

This shift is becoming more evident every day, but it remains incomplete. Companies that want to reform the way they do business face a challenge in convincing their current customers (be that the consumer or the shareholder) to agree. The knee-jerk tendency is to require a business case for any radical shift. Shareholders and analysts want the reassurance of numbers to show that any changes will add value, that is, financial value, as justification. But one must be wary of business cases. For one thing, they are necessarily based on the past. As for future performance, they are more supposition than prediction; a "best guess" that passes for concrete knowledge. When you are talking about change and leadership, as we noted in Chapter 4, there is no map to follow, and intelligent observation is more reliable than the false reassurance of numerical projections. This is particularly true in the case of doing responsible business, which is about being rewarded for doing the right thing, rather than for doing the wrong thing right. Which brings us to the second shortcoming of the business case: it can be constructed to defend any argument. Reality is more complex than any set of numbers. While data, by its apparently objective nature, appears to tell a complete story, it rarely tells the whole truth. It is sufficient to ignore opposing evidence to make the desired case. Statistics are presented in such a way as to justify the position of the presenter. Evidence to the contrary can be just as accurate, reducing the business case for or against a course of action to subjective opinion. The ongoing debate about climate change is one such example. For every convincing body of data presented by a group of experts, skeptics can produce just as convincing a set that can prove the opposite. The future is not provable, and so any business case is, by definition, subjective.

More important than a business case is an understanding of the factors and actions that can create or destroy value. And more important than financial statements is an overall "balance sheet" that takes account of the assets and liabilities in a company's strategy, actions, and relationships beyond its financial transactions. Investment in increasing the whole amount of value available to society provides the greatest returns to an organization. On the other hand, using company resources to benefit only a few stakeholders while squeezing performance at the cost of others is detrimental to organizational health. Providing benefits to parties all along and around the value chain achieves a larger and more sustainable increase in performance and shareholder value. Excessive emphasis on "getting the numbers up," combined with too narrowly distributed gains will, however, erode the organization, with immediate and destructive consequences.

There is no one formula for creating shared value. It requires each organization to develop its own calculation of financial, cultural, and psychological factors to define maximum value creation. Luxury does not follow the same models as most other businesses. It can appear to be based much more on the instinctive and irrational than the planned and quantified. Where most companies compete on price, luxury companies compete by increasing perceived value; all the more reason for luxury firms not to be hamstrung by fear of the unproven.

This gives luxury an important leadership role, because for society to change, new habits must reach a tipping point. The lack of progress in humanizing business practice is because the efforts are still isolated and seen as evangelistic. They must converge into a critical, irresistible mass. In *The Tipping Point*, Malcolm Gladwell describes three types of actors crucial to building the momentum that causes society to change tack;[1] mavens, or experts, enrich society by their need to spread knowledge, connectors are the neuralgic points that serve as platforms for that knowledge to "go viral," while salesmen persuade others to go along through the attractiveness of their charisma. Luxury brands are perfectly placed at the nexus of all three. Further, we pay a disproportionate amount of attention to the world of luxury. Do a Google image search for "airplane interior" and notice the abundance of first-class and private jet cabins that emerges, despite these categories' comparatively small share of the aviation market by volume (not just relative to economy class, but to the vast array of cargo and military aircraft as well). We fantasize about and project ourselves into a world of luxury – whatever that word means to you – which ties luxury to another of Malcolm Gladwell's points: stickiness, or the ability to connect emotionally with and retain a message. So, luxury hits us where it counts. When it comes to transforming the way the world functions, the combination of all these factors means that luxury can push people past the "bystander effect," or the passive witnessing of a problem while expecting someone else to do something about it.

When Yves Saint Laurent masculinized women's wear with pants and smoking jackets, it was more than a new fashion trend. Saint Laurent was picking up on what was going on in the world around him, and turning the prosaic and practical, but inelegant, into something sophisticated and desirable. It was the mid-1960s. Coco Chanel had shocked the world by wearing her lover's clothing in public as early as 1906, but took another 40 years to develop her personal iconoclasm into the signature Chanel skirt suit. André Courrèges had first presented the trouser as part of a designer collection in 1961. But pants were stuck between being a practical tool or a bold style statement. A proper lady would not wear them to an elegant occasion, not even the formality of an office. But Saint Laurent was able to pick up on currents that were still below the surface and had not yet coalesced into a movement. He feminized the masculine codes of the tuxedo by moving the seams and darts to complement the feminine physique, thus allowing the tuxedo to function like a ball gown: rather than flattening a woman's curves the way men's clothing would, Saint Laurent accentuated them. He elevated social currents to the level of haute couture, giving legitimacy to the novelty. Surrounded by his muses, young women from a glamorous yet intellectual beau monde of artists, entertainers, and aristocrats, he had the antennae to pick up on faint social signals and then amplify and rebroadcast them by incorporating pants into the eventual launch of his ready-to-wear collection. Each woman reading *Vogue* was suddenly encouraged and able to make this "radical" movement her own.

The business case for women's trousers would have been impossible to construct. Focus groups would have rejected the hypothetical as too far removed from the consumer's experience. It was only by appropriating them into real life that the demand eventually developed. It was Saint Laurent's intuition and willingness to take a risk as an artist that allowed him to create value for the market in a way that marketers could not.

In simple supply and demand terms, value creation is straightforward. Meet demand at a cost below what the market will bear. This is business as usual, where the fixed and variable costs of production and the required profit are met by the product value a customer is willing to pay for. For luxury goods, there is an additional demand premium based on the perceived value of the good. Customers are willing to pay more for the "privilege" of ownership of something rare and widely desired. Shared value creation allows a company to make this pie bigger by leveraging intangibles outside the production process. By investing in long-term assets such as innovation capacity and networks of supportive relationships, companies see financial returns as well as harder to measure benefits, like creativity, synergies, employee motivation, and productivity, and the proactive management of risks (Figure 7.1).

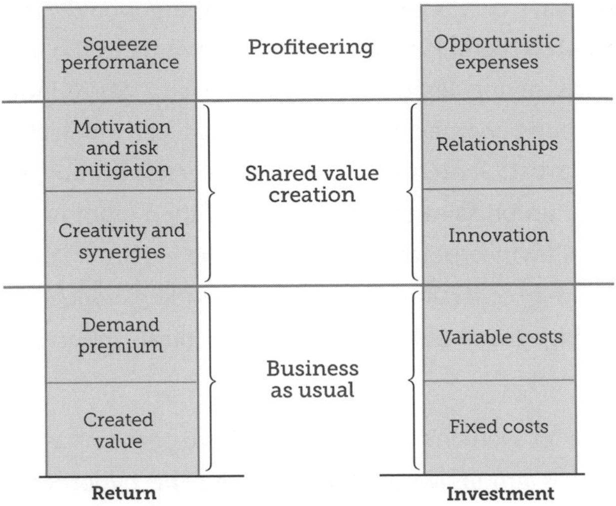

FIGURE 7.1 / Balancing profit and profiteering

Performance versus value creation

Writing in 1997, McKinsey's Ralf Leszinski and Michael Marn focused on the value inherent in a product:[2]

> The real essence of value revolves around the tradeoff between the benefits a customer receives from a product and the price he or she pays for it ... the higher the perceived benefit and/or the lower the price of a product, the higher the customer value and the greater the likelihood that customers will choose that product.

The reference to "perceived benefits" hints at the mutable nature of value in what is important to the customer. Since 1997, consumers have begun looking at larger definitions of value. Perceived costs now include the product's impact on the environment and the community. And perceived benefits now include the overall contribution that a customer's purchase makes to their sense of serenity and wellbeing.

Leszinski and Marn identify a value equivalence line between price and benefits where "you get what you pay for." Typically, companies aim to keep the price low relative to the benefits, setting off a race to the bottom. As we know, luxury works differently. Luxury brands focus on the perceived benefits rather than the price, which sets off a race toward the top. Luxury in particular often uses higher price as a signal of higher benefits, rendering them more exclusive and thus more desirable. This partly explains the 60 percent rise in luxury goods prices over the past decade, compared to general consumer price inflation of about half that rate.[3] But is using price to generate exclusivity consistent with the authenticity that is a crucial factor in the perceived value of a luxury product? Further, what happens when the higher store price is combined with other perceived costs? As consumers become more aware of the externalities of their purchasing behavior, these become a factor in their decision making. And as the increased visibility of luxury brands mixes with a growing worldwide debate about income inequality, consumers shift their perception of value to the innate qualities of the product rather than the highly visible branding that surrounds it. Luxury brands have long depended on the universe they construct around the brand to drive desire. That universe must now create a dialogue between business and social value.

Often, companies will point to job creation as an example of the social or shared value they generate. This is a stretch. While creating jobs is good for the economy, it does not equal the creation of value for society more broadly. In fact, it can even be destructive of social value. In the wake of the financial crisis of 2008 came an increased focus not just on job availability, but also job quality and the fairness of pay structures within companies. This brought unwelcome attention to companies such as Walmart, whose owners' legendary wealth stands in stark contrast to the food drives that some stores organized in support of their own employees.[4] McDonald's also became a magnet for controversy when their employee helpline was reported to have recommended that full-time workers find second jobs and request government welfare assistance to make ends meet.[5] According to one study, by the end of 2013, McDonald's, the quintessentially American brand, were the most hated company in America.[6]

Luxury brands do not play the same low-cost, low-margin game as companies like Walmart and McDonald's. With the consolidation of luxury firms into big corporations, luxury is drifting in this direction, but this danger is still far off. Nonetheless, luxury brands do play a similar reputational game as mass-market brands. Their brand recognition and their need to be looked up to and admired by wide swaths of the market in order to flourish put them in the same category. While the masses may not buy their products, it is the mass aspiration to their products that provides the validation to those who do.

So, while luxury brands are known for providing good working conditions and other labor practices, they should be aware that simple job creation is not enough. Luxury brands highlight their provision of manufacturing jobs in Europe at a time when most of these are being outsourced to developing countries. But even this is not enough. Beyond the fact that a successful business cannot exist without labor, the perceived quality and thus the location of that labor is important for a luxury brand. The customer for French luxury brands demands that the product be made in France. Outsourcing these jobs would decrease the value of the brand. So, job creation is not the creation of social value, it is a prerequisite for the brand's own value. While it may be commendable, it is nothing more than business as usual. To create shared value, the job created has to promote relevant and vital knowledge that contributes to the community's long-term autonomy. So, assembling a watch in Switzerland from parts manufactured in China in order to call it "Made in Switzerland" is not the same as having the intellectual and technological capability to conceive, design, and manufacture all the elements from start to finish in one place.

A similar story can be told about growth and financial performance. The rates of growth and profitability are seen as a litmus test for the health of a company. It is difficult to suggest to a company's executives that they are on the wrong track when they can point to a long track record of financial success. But financial success is only evidence of financial success, not of value creation. There are many ways to achieve financial success. Bernard Madoff is a case in point: a multimillionaire, a respected business leader, a highly sought-after investment advisor with an exclusive client roster of respected funds and famous individuals. And all this success was based on history's biggest Ponzi scheme, which even government investigators could not discern from a legitimate business. Without going to the extremes of crime, Wall Street firms saw tremendous growth in size and profits in the period following deregulation in the 1980s. Their scale and apparent stability, however, did nothing to prevent and may even have exacerbated the financial crisis of 2008, the largest since financial regulation had begun in earnest 70 years prior. The problem was that the pursuit of profitability and growth ignored the underlying fundamentals of business activity and its broader repercussions on the economy and society. In the particular case of 2008, the problem stemmed from helping consumers into homeownership, which was seen as good for business and good for society as well. But the ability to make money from home loans created a frenzy that quickly exceeded the pool of people able to pay back those loans. Eventually, the scheme collapsed, setting off a chain reaction of financial and business failures. The business model, based on the supposedly objective evidence of money, had exceeded the value it provided.

Companies need to maximize profits. Nobody is arguing against that. But while this seems like a simple concept, the notion of maximization is actually subjective because it depends on what one considers as reasonable costs. A company's processes and culture determine the definition of reasonable. A mass consumer goods company may find it wasteful to spend money on exotic travel for their creative teams or building a collection of art and antiques. A luxury brand, on the other hand, may allow it as an important source of research and inspiration that contributes to the brand's unique artistic capacity. Even companies within the same field can differ on these perspectives depending on their organizational values. One company may see an executive jet as a wasteful extravagance, while another sees it as a necessary tool for their executives' flexibility and efficiency.

The drive to maximize efficiency and profits can easily become counterproductive. The common cubicle provides one example of this. The cubicle was developed in the 1960s as a step-up from open-plan offices. Until then, secretarial pools and clerical workers occupied vast, classroom-like spaces of aligned desks, with managers in private offices. In the 1990s, organizational psychologists promoted cubicles as a way to flatten hierarchies, and improve collaboration, communication, and productivity. While these were the selling points to employees, it was also true that companies could see considerable savings on their facilities' expenses by eliminating space-consuming individual offices. Today, about 70 percent of offices rely on cubicles or open floor plans.[7] Twenty years of research has shown the disruptive effects of cubicles on productivity and the false savings that result. Technology has mostly taken over clerical and secretarial functions. Vast typing pools are a thing of the past. The new occupants of these spaces are more senior, substantive workers, performing analytical, strategic, creative, and sales roles, which would have been carried out in private offices, or smaller setups shared by collaborating teams. Other than spaces like design studios or trading floors where constant interaction between employees is crucial, cubicles have been found to cause higher level of stress and distraction and lower levels of satisfaction and motivation among employees. Noise pollution and the lack of privacy are the chief concerns. While the idea was to facilitate communication, it has more often had the opposite effect by making workers self-conscious about being overheard.[8]

Think about it: where do you do your best work? In a quiet, private, comfortable space where you can focus your thoughts, have sensitive discussions, and adapt your environment to suit your needs, or in a vast sea of uniform stations subject to ringing phones, the conversations of others, and lighting and temperature completely out of your control? We adapt, of course, because we have to get the job done. But when we spend our energy adapting, we are diverting our energy from getting the job done.

The cubicle is an example of the false promise of the business case. While it is easy to make the arguments for immediate cost savings, the detrimental effects take longer to realize. What is more, companies cannot compare their actual performance with the unrealized gains. The only way would be to undertake the costs of converting office space to new formats and wait for the results. While we can register the dissatisfaction of workers today, how does one make the case for investment in uncertain future results? The answer, as we have argued all along in this book, is to refocus attention from the financial or the institutional to the individual. There are no secrets here because we can draw from the intuition that is a product of our own experiences and the interpersonal relationships we live with all day, every day. Neither are there neat organizational tricks of the kind that companies and especially management consultants like to promote. For all the attention given to lauded efficiency management tools such Six Sigma, they ultimately encourage a race to the bottom by reducing human beings to cogs in a machine. Machines do not undertake new thinking. Mechanical processes do not give people a sense of meaning or personal fulfillment. These are crucial to the innovation and motivation that allow organizations to thrive. Rules and quotas are important for benchmarking performance, but they do not generate the energy that drives a company forward. Instead, they lead to prudence and risk aversion; avoiding sanction rather than pursuing reward. Stifling creativity and individual engagement erodes the performance of an organization and its ability to create value over the longer term. Despite the masses of data that now highlight the shortcomings of open-plan offices, they do not tell us anything that we do not already know from life experience. Managers who have ignored this have simply allowed quick wins to trump long-term interests.

Value creation means focusing on what matters to individuals, and not just to systems. Systems, whatever their functional purpose, are designed to serve people. Take the example of the BMW production line for senior workers, which we described in Chapter 5. In redesigning the production line, BMW listened to workers about their optimal working conditions. BMW also worked with experts in physiology and ergonomics to take account of how those needs would evolve in the future as the workers continued to age. Second, BMW learned to apply this knowledge to other production lines and found that it increased productivity, reduced absenteeism and other costs across the manufacturing infrastructure. This illustrates that BMW do not just provide value by making automobiles. They recognize that the whole of the organization exists to serve people. As a luxury brand, BMW's interests are best served by finding ways to imbue their whole system with value rather than cutting costs. They could have argued that an aging population is a rationale for outsourcing jobs, even if the BMW customer values the "Made in Germany" status of their cars. Instead, BMW recognized that their older workers are an important repository of skills and institutional memory. Further, with European governments raising retirement ages, BMW recognized the need to look after the wellbeing of the population by continuing to provide economic opportunities. By serving their own people, they improved how they serve people on the outside as well.

The perils of financialization

Share price has become the single most important indicator of a company's performance. The right of shareholders to demand the highest possible returns on their investment has even assumed a quasi-legal legitimacy with the corporate governance regulations that are now imposed on publicly traded firms. This reveals the dark side of a system ostensibly meant to ensure the responsible running of a corporation. Through corporate governance regulations, shareholders can effectively impose a legal obligation on a company to put their interests first. Groups of shareholders can sue against what they perceive as the mismanagement of share price (as opposed to mismanagement of the company) and even against the reinvestment of revenues rather than their distribution to shareholders as dividends. In the words of Lynn Stout, professor of law at Cornell University, this is a dictatorship by shareholders, which proves unfounded once companies go bust.[9] Stout points out that in a bankruptcy, shareholders are the last claimants considered, only getting what assets remain after all other liabilities are settled.

According to McKinsey:

> Executives overburdened by the demands of their companies' short-term investors may yearn for a more supportive crowd that might be less skittish about volatility. Such investors would base their decisions on a deeper understanding of a company's strategy,

performance, and potential to create long-term value – and would not pressure a company for short-term gains at the expense of greater long-term growth.[10]

The drive for efficiency, the domination of business case thinking, comes from the changing relationship between businesses and their shareholders. Individual shareholders were an important part of stock markets in the first half of the 20th century. This was the way many of our grandparents invested when they bought shares in Coca-Cola or IBM. People bought stocks as a form of savings and held them for a long time, believing that as companies grew, so would their investment. Because they were individuals, a company's shareholders, employees, and customers were more closely aligned in their interests. A shareholder who is also a consumer of a company's products has a personal relationship with the brand. In a sense, they were built-in quality controllers with a first-hand understanding of how the brand experience – the quality of its products, its customer service, its reputation in the marketplace – affects the returns on their investment. If you do not like a company as a customer, why would you have any faith in its future as an owner?

This dynamic changed as financial markets got bigger and more sophisticated. Fewer people buy shares of a company directly; instead, their money is invested through institutions, such as mutual or pension funds, or managed wealth accounts. While there have always been wealthy individuals and institutions that controlled a large portion of a company's shares, their influence was balanced by the broad sea of ordinary people, who, together, held an even bigger stake. In the 1950s, institutional investors controlled only 7 percent of equities in the US and far less in other countries.[11] By the 2000s, that proportion had risen to more than 60 percent in the US, and as high as 80 percent in other countries.[12] With this change came a different attitude toward the running of companies. While individuals can feel a personal bond to the companies they invest in, institutions are dispassionate owners, interested only in the numbers and the level of their returns on investment. Individuals can be engaged to get behind a long-term vision of the brand, a transformation for the better. Institutions are more interested in efficiency and the bottom line. As owners, they are less concerned by far off potential than they are about immediate results. And they are quick to go where the returns are right now.

By various estimates, the average length of share ownership in companies has decreased from about five years in the 1960s to about 22 seconds today. While this last number is hotly contested, even the most conservative analyses push the number only as high as about seven months. Whether it is seconds or months, the implication is the same: companies that focus on their share price are simply incapable of executing long-term strategy. This is the stick in the wheels that prevents companies from evolving and considering, let alone adopting, more socially useful business practices. It is at the core of the split between a company's ability to combine business value and social value, by pitting stakeholders against one another and undermining their ability to focus on common objectives.

The drop in the duration of share ownership is an unintended result of financialization. Financialization came about from the deregulation of banking and financial market activities in the 1970s and 80s, particularly in Britain and the US. It encouraged more speculative investment, leveraged with borrowed money, rather than the investment of a shareholder's existing assets. This added the pressure of repayment periods to investors' demands for the performance of a company's shares. Hedge funds and high-frequency trading have supplanted the dominance of individual and institutional investors in financial markets and true equity investment in companies. The difference is that hedge funds and high-frequency traders have no interest in the underlying business of a company. They are only interested in fluctuations of the share price, and have the incentive to drive that price as high as possible as fast as possible before they get out. What happens to the company afterwards does not matter to them. High-frequency traders, in particular, move into and out of large blocks of shares in seconds, relying on a favorable move of only a few cents to make their gains. In contrast, individual investors and institutions such as pension funds hold company shares for the long term. They look at the business fundamentals, the market potential, and the capacity for sound, sane, responsible management. While somewhat different, private equity firms typically take stakes in companies they feel they can grow or improve. They too have an interest in the business itself, not just manipulation of the share price.

In Chapter 2, we discussed the effect on luxury when control of a firm passes from a designer or artisan to a team of managers and financiers. Ideally, they should both support the same vision of value creation. Unfortunately, too often the focus shifts from creation to efficiency and expansion. If making a sale is your primary purpose, you become obliged to follow the market, whereas if you are driven by the expression of a purpose, you are more likely to respond to the market by leading it. As luxury companies engage private equity and hire management experts to run the company, this distinction gets further complicated by the difference between an owner who manages their company and has a personal stake in its evolution, versus a salaried manager (even one with stock options) whose stake is purely financial. Finally, as we describe above, the entrance of investors who are less interested in the fundamental activity than the externalities of profit and share price that that activity brings can cause luxury companies to drift quite far from the values and vision that determine their mission. So, for luxury companies, it is particularly important – and even more so as they turn to financial markets as a source of capital – to leverage their culture as an asset in order to attract not just investors, but the right investors.

In October 2013, Michael Dell did something radical. In the era of high-profile technology initial public offerings – the same year as Twitter and a year after Facebook – and frenzied interest in Apple and Google, he spent $25 billion to buy back the shares of Dell Computers, one of the biggest PC makers, and take the company off the stock exchange. Dell had always been an innovator. His home-based business of assembling and shipping computers himself directly to customers quickly grew to rival IBM and Hewlett-Packard in the PC market. But by 2013, with the emergence of new technology and the convergence of computer, web and mobile platforms, that market was in decline. Dell needed to innovate again and restructure the company to focus on services and software. Dell Computers' public listing, the goal of every high-tech startup, was the main barrier. The requirement of pleasing shareholders and maintaining the stock price was hampering the company's ability to take the risks needed to evolve with the times. Commenting on Carl Icahn, his largest shareholder and main opponent in the buyback, Michael Dell said:

> It's a big poker game to him … It's not about the customers. It's not about the people. It's not about changing the world. He doesn't give a crap about any of that. He didn't know whether we made nuclear power plants or French fries. He didn't care.[13]

The Dell story illustrates the importance of a company aligning the vision of shareholders and managers with their purpose. They must understand the product in terms of "why" and "how" before they understand it as a "what." This is not an argument against professional management or public listing. Much maligned by socially minded activists, public listing can actually be an important guarantor of good corporate governance and accountability. Rather, it means that a company's shareholders and bosses should be attuned to the company's values, vision, and purpose, rather than just their ability to churn out products that yield quick returns. Companies talk about branding to attract and retain customers. They talk about employer branding to attract and retain employees. But what about their shareholder branding and their ability to attract and retain investors? This responsibility is left to CFOs and investor relations teams, who focus on the objective evidence of cost and revenue management. This disconnects the flow of money, the lifeblood of the business, from the origins of its activity.

If the money and not the value is seen as the primary driver of the business, it forces all other aspects to fall in line. The values of the company then become about making money rather than serving a need. The company's vision becomes one of itself, blinkered, rather than one of the marketplace or the world. And its mission becomes to reap profits and grow. Few consumers would support this mission if it were stated bluntly, so companies create a second, external personality in order to attract them. Here lies the essential tension between which customer to serve – the shareholder or the consumer – which finds management and employees caught in the middle. No wonder, then, that companies have to create a third face, which masks this tension and explains to staff the advantages designed for them. We now have three demands on the company's resources pulling it in different directions. As one entity, one brand to all these stakeholders, companies need to formulate one multifaceted value proposition that satisfies them all. This means not just attracting and retaining investors, but getting the right investors to support its purpose and see it through challenges with consistency and committed leadership.

Toward a healthier organization

Not all investors are created equal. It is not true that all investors are only interested in consistently positive cash flow and profitability. These are ultimately necessary for a company's health, but they can be managed over a long-term arc that understands and accepts quarterly volatility in the pursuit of durable success. Aled Smith, who manages the Global Leaders Fund and the American Fund at M&G Investments, says it seems that a lot of investors "aren't prepared to admit that the world will still exist in five years, so they want to get their money back sooner."[14] He points out that these investors tend to ignore companies that allow the importance of making long-term investments to trump the need to avoid short-term disruptions. He says it is more important to look for companies that cultivate continuous improvement.

Further, the image of the profit-at-all-costs capitalist is receding as the importance of sustainability and social consciousness percolate through society. Sustainable and socially responsible investment funds and market indexes are gaining popularity and eschewing companies – even highly profitable ones   in industries like oil, tobacco, and arms that are not aligned with the objective of creating a better world. Social enterprises are finding their footing and attracting capital with their efforts to solve problems, not just reap benefits. As time goes on, demand for ethical business will increase on the part of consumers, and the long tail of investors will follow suit. Y Combinator, a high-tech investor and incubator in Silicon Valley, have made a "no assholes" rule popular among a certain set of tech companies, encouraging them to develop civilized workplaces.[15] According to Paul Graham, Y Combinator's head:

> It's certainly possible to build a multibillion dollar startup without being a jerk ... In fact, based on what I've seen so far, the good people have the advantage over the jerks. Probably because to get

really big, a company has to have a sense of mission, and the good people are more likely to have an authentic one, rather than just being motivated by money or power.

Cultivating the right culture shared among employees, managers, investors, and customers is a crucial part of creating what Scott Keller and Colin Price refer to as "organizational health." In *Beyond Performance: How Great Organizations Build Ultimate Competitive Advantage*, Keller and Price define organizational health as "the ability of your organization to align, execute, and renew itself" faster than the competition.[16] They identify three factors particularly important to organizational health, all of which derive from a company's culture rather than being based on its performance objectives. These factors are motivation, external orientation, and coordination and control.[17] The authors write: "Amazing contributions don't come from employees who feel like conscripts ... passion is the difference between 'insipid' and 'inspired'." In addition, to avoid being insipid, a company must be attuned to the rapid and complex changes happening in its environment. Otherwise, its ideas will be outdated before they are even implemented. Finally, the ability to be passionate and responsive is a direct result of management style. If people's work is too tightly controlled, managers become enforcers rather than linchpins connecting complex systems. What Keller and Price call "managing without managers" seeks to push control to the periphery as a framework within which people have the self-governance to determine the best way to get the job done while making sure the system is still coherent as a whole. Getting and staying healthy involves tending to the people-oriented aspects of leading an organization. These only lend themselves to a business case if that case includes the shared value of social responsibility.

McKinsey found that, while stakeholders support social responsibility, they also are vigilant that such initiatives should not encroach on the company's performance.[18] For example, they found that more social responsibility led to improved consumer engagement only when a company's products were considered to be of superior quality. A company with lower quality products actually lost consumer interest by pushing their social responsibility agenda. This sets up a counterpoint to earlier luxury research findings, which showed that luxury brands should avoid too close a link between their product and social value propositions. Some marketers had found that the self-indulgent aspect of luxury could clash with the feelings that some consumers experience when confronted with social causes. This created feelings of guilt, which discouraged the purchase. Luxury brands are, by definition, superior, so they have little downside to raising their social value proposition. But they must be careful in establishing the link between the two. The pursuit of social value should not present a contrast to luxury. Rather, they must move the person's emotions in the same direction. Rather than feeling guilty about their purchase of a luxury good, or feeling indifferent (such as when no link is made), the consumer can actually feel good about their buying decision through internal and external validation. The McKinsey research identified three principles for helping social responsibility drive value for the firm:

1 *Do not hide market motives.* Stakeholders are open to social responsibility as long as it makes sense with the company's business activity and is pursued with authentic intent rather than as a marketing opportunity.
2 *Provide tangible benefits.* This applies to the product and the social responsibility effort, in that they must both demonstrate how they live up to the promised value.
3 *Evaluate progress.* This allows a company to make sure that its product and social value propositions are and remain aligned over time.

An example is Chanel's purchase of embroiderer Lesage and milliner Maison Michel. The acquisition of these artisanal firms served to reinforce Chanel's pool of highly specialized skills, necessary for their core couture business. At the same time, the acquisition also helped preserve two firms important to French cultural heritage by helping them continue to survive. This was not simple vertical integration. The two houses were not absorbed into Chanel and put at the larger company's exclusive service. They continue to work with their client roster, even brands that compete with Chanel. Chanel do not tie themselves to single-handedly provide for the smaller firms' continued existence. Lesage's ongoing evolution and collaboration with other houses is the benchmark of this endeavor's success. Whether one sees this as an act of cultural magnanimity or a smart business move is up to the observer. Chanel are clearly a winner on both counts.

This alignment between business and social value is key to support a value-oriented business model. Doug Conant is chairman of the Committee Encouraging Corporate Philanthropy and nonexecutive chairman of Avon Products. He sees corporate philanthropy as a tool for research and development in addition to a tool for social responsibility. According to Conant, corporate philanthropy can be "a discovery phase in investment in a social issue" and thus forms a laboratory for experimenting with ideas that address community and corporate needs.[19] It allows companies to explore investment in activities where the returns are uncertain. He cites examples of companies such as Vodaphone, which solved a socioeconomic problem that aligned with their mission in order to create new growth areas for their business. Vodaphone used philanthropy to fund a mobile banking initiative in Kenya, building a platform for individual economic empowerment in an underserved community. This eventually turned into a viable market for their Safaricom affiliate. Compare this initiative to Fabergé's Big Egg Hunt, which raised a fortune, but for causes unrelated to the company's mission, leveraging their star power in support of an issue, but not their core competence nor the synergies they share with their stakeholders.

Vacheron Constantin, maker of prestige watches since 1755 and now part of the Richemont group, supports the Rheumasearch Foundation for clinical and fundamental research conducted in the rheumatology department of the University Hospitals of Geneva, as well as the rheumatology laboratory of the Geneva Faculty of Medicine. Rheumatic disorders, which affect millions of people worldwide, are particularly debilitating for watchmakers, who need precise control of their hands to be able to work on a microscopic level. Thus, there is a direct link between the core purpose of the brand and its philanthropic work. As Doug Conant illustrates with Vodafone, Vacheron Constantin's support of rheumatology research contributes to the company's own work and is a major concern of their stakeholder community. Further, Vacheron Constatin helped to launch the Barbier-Mueller Museum Cultural Foundation, dedicated to testifying to little-known cultures in order to preserve the essential elements of their myths, traditions, and sociopolitical organization. Watchmaking as a profession is particularly tied to skills transmitted over generations to the point where watchmaking communities in Switzerland have evolved such specific methods that they cannot be outsourced to the neighboring valley, let alone globalized. According to Vacheron Constantin: "The duty of passing on knowledge is a core concern of watchmaking itself. Because watchmaking as we know it is first and foremost a cultural phenomenon."[20] Beyond preserving a quaint tradition, the transmission of knowledge is essential to the diversity and richness of human civilization.

Luxury brands are leaders. Knowing how to lead them appropriately is essential. While the business case may be reassuring, it is ultimately a crutch that prevents organizations from exploring a wide range of opportunities to create value and thus stymies their capacity for innovation and leadership. The history of luxury shows that every successful luxury brand has been founded on a vision and driven by instinct that is ultimately sensitive to and designed to serve people.

Notes

1   Gladwell, M. (2002) *The Tipping Point: How Little Things Can Make a Big Difference.* Back Bay Books.

2   Leszinski, R. and Marn, M. (1997) "Setting value, not price". *McKinsey Quarterly*, February.

3   Sherman, L. (2013) "Fashion inflation: Why are prices rising so fast?" *The Business of Fashion*, August 2.

4   Halloran, L. (2013) "Wal-Mart food drive unwittingly fuels talk of minimum wage hike". *NPR*, November 22.

5   Pierson, D. (2013) "McDonald's McResources line urges worker to seek federal assistance". *Los Angeles Times*, October 23.

6   McIntyre, D. (2014) "The 10 most hated companies in America." *24/7 Wall Street*, January 10.

7   Konnikova, M. (2014) "The open-office trap." *The New Yorker*, January 7.

8   Fayard, A.-L. and Weeks, W. (2011) "Who moved my cube?" *Harvard Business Review*, 89(7/8): 102–10.

9   Stout, L. (2012) *The Shareholder Value Myth: How Putting Shareholders First Harms Investors, Corporations, and the Public.* Berrett-Koehler.

10 Palter, R.N., Rehm, W. and Shih, J. (2008) "Communicating with the right investors." *McKinsey Quarterly*, April.

11 Chen, X., Harford, J. and Li, K. (2007) "Monitoring: Which institutions matter?" *Journal of Financial Economics*, 86(2): 279–305.

12 OECD (2011) "The role of institutional investors in promoting good corporate governance." *Corporate Governance.* OECD Publishing.

13 Guglielmo, C. (2013) "Dell officially goes private: Inside the nastiest tech buyout ever." *Forbes*, November 18.

14 Goedhart, M. and Koller, T. (2013) "How to attract long-term investors: An interview with M&G's Aled Smith." *McKinsey Quarterly*, June.

15 Shontell, A. (2014) "Why so many tech founders who are jerks become insanely rich and successful." *Business Insider*, January 18.

16 Keller, S. and Price, C. (2011) *Beyond Performance: How Great Organizations Build Ultimate Competitive Advantage.* Wiley.

17 Hamel, G. and Price, C. (2011) "Creating inspired, open, and free organizations." *Harvard Business Review*, October 12.

18   Bhattacharya, C.B., Korshun, D. and Sen, S. (2011) "What really drives value in corporate responsibility?" *McKinsey Quarterly*, December.

19   Conant, D. (2013) "Why philanthropy is R&D for business." *McKinsey Quarterly*, September.

20   www.vacheron-constantin.com/en5/our-commitments/barbier-mueller-museum-cultural-foundation.

8

The outlook for luxury

• Heritage is more than history. Age alone will not protect luxury brands from the crop of newcomers whose emergence is fueled by a changing global balance and technological revolution.

• Luxury brands must constantly adapt to a "new normal," including the morphing of values brought about by globalization, the fragmentation of geographic communities, and their reorganization by cultural affinity, which combine to change the meaning of luxury.

• Luxury brands can choose to continue practicing business as usual while they wait and see how the world evolves, or they can participate in the change and shape the world. This decision will determine whether they are followers or leaders.

In 2014, researchers at Princeton University published a study predicting the decline of Facebook. Picking up on the migration of younger users away from Facebook to new social networks, and using models from epidemiology and the decline of Myspace as a case study, they concluded that Facebook would lose 80 percent of their users within three years.[1] But epidemics decline because disease is not useful to the individual host organism, although it may be useful for the evolution of the ecosystem, and because it ultimately destroys its host and loses its means of support. For a disease to flourish, it must always be moving on to new and fertile ground because it is competing for survival with its own host. Businesses (ideally) do not aim to destroy their markets. They compete with one another. Myspace declined because their competitor, Facebook, offered a better alternative – it was more useful – just as Myspace had done in their day to Friendster. Friendster had harkened the arrival of social networking by allowing people to build profiles and share content with their network of contacts. But Friendster are now a shell of themselves, focused on online gaming. You can log into Friendster by using your Facebook account. So, a company, unlike a disease, can intervene in its evolution on its own behalf by continuing to be useful to the "host" and evolving along with it. If Facebook are losing users, they have two options. They can act like a disease and try to conquer new markets with the same methods. Or evolve with their market to continue to be useful and relevant to its needs.

After growing rapidly for almost three decades, the revenue growth of established luxury brands is now slowing. While luxury brands remain cautiously optimistic, they cannot ignore the cyclical nature of every business model, and must prepare themselves for the possibility of an approaching decline. Luxury brands cannot rely on their traditional markets for sure growth. During the 2008 crisis, these proved themselves to be unreliable. Neither can they depend on current, emerging markets, as these are also demonstrating the limits of their growth potential. Further, new competitors are emerging from the broad range of independent, niche, sustainable, high-tech, artisanal, and other, smaller and more nimble brands, which now have access to global markets. So, established luxury brands have two options. They can act like a disease and try to conquer new markets with the same methods. Or they can evolve with their market and continue to be useful and relevant to its needs. So far, luxury brands have opted for the first. They have expanded the familiar language of heritage, craftsmanship, creativity, and quality to new territories. It has been their roots in Europe that made their success in Asia. They were already quite established in the Americas and Australia. Now, some are talking about Africa. And after that? Antarctica? What happens when they inevitably run out of new markets to conquer? And, more importantly, how do they revive and protect the markets they already have. They should bear in mind that heritage is no secret weapon. The origin of many of today's most respected brands – Christian Dior, the Ritz hotels, the *Orient Express* – was when they burst onto the scene, unknown but with revolutionary ideas. They are part of the establishment now, but they started out as iconoclasts. So, today's old luxury brands should not be complacent about their birthright.

Speaking at *Luxury Daily*'s Luxury FirstLook: Strategy 2014 conference, Renaud Dutreil, the former chairman of LVMH in the US, said that emerging brands lack the heritage needed for luxury status.[2] According to Dutreil:

> Culture is something that is less visible in the new generation of designers … The result is that they can be very creative because it's an expression of personality … but after five years they are exhausted because they do not have the same access to human culture.

This is true, but luxury brands should not mistake age for a panacea. The long history of an established brand certainly provides it with a richer pool of stories to tell. But this is only one of the resources that a luxury brand has at its disposal, and the value of a resource is in how you use it. If young designers do not have staying power, it is because the story they tell is about themselves and does not take into account the universe in which they work. This danger is equally present for established brands. If they use the resource of heritage to retell stories about the past, they are just respinning old yarns, which charms for a moment but demonstrates nostalgia rather than relevance. Or, if they pick up on the superficial, immediate trends of today, they are actually telling one story but acting according to another. This may make them relevant in the immediate present but undermines their authenticity and trustworthiness over the long term. Neither do they connect with the deeper social and cultural currents, as did Yves Saint Laurent, for example. It is the brand's ability to understand and respond to the deeper currents rather than stylistic ploys that, as we have demonstrated in multiple ways in this book, will allow a brand to stay relevant over time.

Companies can choose to wait until the market shifts and then respond, or they can lead. This should not be a foreign concept to companies used to generating demand for their products. The difference is that they will have to take a position on what they are leading their stakeholders to, beyond just getting them to buy more products. They will have to propose a vision of the kind of world they are contributing to, and explain their mission in creating that world. The customer will then choose whether or not to support that vision – and the brand via the vision – based on their own worldview in a sort of consumer election process.

This means an opportunity and a challenge for luxury brands. Those that have a long history of cultural continuity and respect will outperform those perceived as opportunistic and easily swayed by the whims of fashion. While this highlights the importance of a brand's heritage, it is not a vision of the past. It is not the charm of history or nostalgia. Rather, it is a track record of having a consistent vision for the future, of innovating, solving problems, challenging old notions. In this sense, heritage is the opposite of what we think of as heritage. More than history, it is the depth of their persuasion, the authenticity of their words, and the coherence in their behaviors – all their behaviors – that matter most. Companies that have spent their time scampering in every direction to be popular rather than staying the course by investing in their intellect and their practice will find their job increasingly difficult. They will find that a long history of trendiness does not, in the end, add up to brand equity. They will find that endlessly reinterpreting their archives does not, in the end, add up to innovation. They will find that their customers are fickle, addicted to novelty, and ready to drop them for the new, new thing.

From "business as usual" to "the new normal"

Ever since the financial meltdown of 2008 led to a global economic crisis, the world has been anticipating the return of business as usual. But business as usual never existed. At best, it is a near-sighted vision of the past. The world and business have been in constant evolution. Thanks to the crisis, our vision of the future evolved as well. Remember, the words "crisis" and "decision" share the same etymological origins. It is the point at which we assess, learn, and move forward in new directions. Figure 8.1 illustrates this evolution, which results when economic shifts lead to new values and patterns of behavior. Returning to business as usual would be a wasted opportunity, a repetition of old mistakes. The closest we can get to business as usual is by creating a company and a brand based on deep, essential values: a vision of the world and its purpose within that world, where its fundamentals remain constant over time. The closest we can get to business as usual is to remain true to ourselves, no matter what is going on around us.

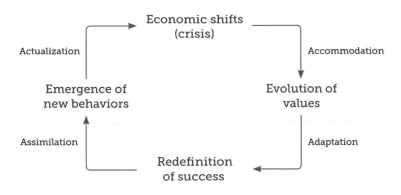

FIGURE 8.1 The socioeconomic cycle

The 2008 crisis was a turning point. It was a convergence of old habits with new possibilities that resulted in a perfect storm. It brought us deeper knowledge of our systems, our institutions, our leaders, and ourselves. The crisis shifted the weight of economic power on earth. Catastrophe in developed regions was offset by opportunities in emerging markets. One could imagine the earth's axis of rotation changing its angle and the dramatic upheaval that would cause. It is a reminder to developed, Western countries that the exalted status they have enjoyed for over a century is not a birthright. History will be quick to remind us that China, India, and the Middle East had sophisticated civilizations and refined cultures while Europeans were still struggling through the material and intellectual poverty of the Dark Ages and before the existence of the Americas was even known to them. Today we debate whether it is possible for a luxury brand to come from China. The heritage of luxury is French, Italian, and British, right? But not so long ago, the luxuries these countries enjoyed – silk, spices, carpets, jewels – came from China, India, and the Middle East. Europeans were just the ones who turned up with the gold (and eventually the guns) they used to get them. If we are to understand how today's cash-laden, emerging, luxury customers are going to evolve, we should look at the evolution of luxury in the West, which went from buying it to appropriating it, transforming it, and eventually creating it.

But this is about more than the simple redistribution of wealth and an indication of the sources of the world's new crop of luxury consumers. The balance of economic power also sets the tone for the evolution of social values, cultural practices, and even consumer tastes. Reconstruction after World War II spread US culture around the globe. The most obvious symbols are the consumer brands. Disney, Coca-Cola, and Levi's developed a vast, global presence. These brands were accompanied by American management culture, with its emphasis on free markets and leveraged investment. Once an American invention, MBAs are now offered by universities around the world and top American schools compete with others for international prestige. The brands also brought new tastes and values. Fast food caught on in countries with a long and intricate tradition of cuisine. As a result, America's obesity epidemic is now appearing in Europe and Asia.

In modern times, globalization has resembled Americanization. But that will change as increasingly diverse influences are added to the mix. China's immunity to the global economic crisis sets pundits off in praise of a more tightly controlled economy. Japan's Uniqlo now have flagship stores on New York's Fifth Avenue and Paris's Place de l'Opéra. Luxury firms have taken an interest and a stake in brands like Qeelin, the Chinese fine jewelry brand bought by Kering in 2013, or Shang Xia, the Chinese luxury brand launched by Hermès. Beginning in 2011, a spate of Asian hotel companies cemented their legitimacy as worldwide luxury brands, with Mandarin Oriental, Raffles, Shangri-La, and Peninsula debuting acclaimed properties at Paris's most prestigious addresses. India's Taj Hotels Resorts and Palaces took over New York's iconic The Pierre hotel in 2005. The arrival of Asian hospitality culture in the West raised the bar for guest service in these markets. Chinese, Japanese, and Korean movies show in European multiplex cinemas, as European movies gain traction in the US, whereas foreign films were once confined to festivals and independent art house theaters.

With this multiplication of influences, perceptions of and esteem for national cultures will evolve as well. Since World War I, the US was seen as the world's protector, a benevolent force acting in the name of freedom and democracy against aggressive and oppressive regimes. By 2013, however, a WIN/Gallup poll of people in 65 countries revealed the US as the biggest perceived threat to world peace, well ahead of less globally trusted states such as China, Iran, and North Korea.[3] Where developed countries could once dictate economic policy to the developing world, newly empowered emerging markets now bristle at dictates and advice they deem condescending coming from New York, London, or Paris, and even international bodies like the World Bank or the IMF. If all countries once wanted to emulate the prosperity and development of the West, more and more countries demand recognition of their own values, traditions, and specific economic conditions; their attitudes towards money, the environment, and people.

If Europe has for some time been seen as the crucible of luxury, it no longer has the monopoly on all things refined. Countries are rediscovering the value and depth of their own traditions and learning to see homegrown luxury on an equal footing with today's revered brands. Even European luxury consumers, growing bored with familiar and omnipresent luxury brands, are seeking out the exotic and rare. This is an unsurprising consequence of the natural condition of luxury. Luxury is what we do not have and is hard to get. Luxury is always ahead of us, so luxury firms cannot afford to fall behind.

To think of the world order we have grown up with as permanent is naive and leaves us unprepared to handle the dynamic and shifting reality. According to the OECD, by 2030, China and the US will have traded places in terms of their shares of the world economy.[4] The US will shrink from 23 to 18%, while China will approach 28%. India will surpass the US by 2060, having traded places with the eurozone, which will have fallen from 17% of world GDP today to 12% and then 9% between 2030 and 2060. Japan faces a similar crisis as Europe, both affected by aging populations. This does not mean that economies will shrink, but rather that, as the world economy grows, the gains will be distributed differently than they were before. Per person incomes in developed and emerging countries will move closer together. While the gap between rich and poor countries will be smaller in 2060, today's rich countries can still take heart that they will not have been displaced in the overall ranking. Wealth is like water. As national barriers drop in the face of globalization, it will eventually find its common level across countries, even as it polarizes within them.

The populations of Dubai, Shanghai, Mumbai, Lagos, São Paulo, and myriad other cities across the world have seen explosive population growth over the past decade, paralleling the growth of their economic fortunes. The influx has not just been armies of provincial workers coming to build shopping malls. As these cities have come onto the world stage, a class of international executives has been drawn to their energy and opportunities from the traditional power centers of New York, London, and Paris. At the same time, new elites in the emerging cities are drawn to the prestige of the new "Old World." Studies of Chinese millionaires in 2013 found that over half (as many as 70 percent according to some research) have either emigrated or plan to do so, mostly to the US and Europe.[5] The arrival of wealthy Chinese, Indians, Russians, and Arabs is driving up luxury real estate prices in major cities in Europe and the US. The combination of the two international flows is leading to what economist Martin Wolf calls a "global plutocracy," "ever more detached from the countries that produced them."[6] Detachment can breed indifference and insularity. This is one of the criticisms directed at corporations, governments, and organizations, which seem incapable or, worse, uninterested in giving more than lip service to the concerns of the vast majority of citizens.

The implications of this are explosive: inequality will no longer be a developing country phenomenon. It will be a worldwide condition, with a single, interconnected global elite, similar to preindustrial times or, indeed, many futurist scenarios in movies and literature. In early 2014, the World Economic Forum (WEF) highlighted the systemic risks the world is facing.[7] A continuation of the environmental factors we discussed in Chapter 3, they also point to the longer term transition that the 2008 crisis catalyzed. Among the highest concern and highest likelihood, the WEF points to those risks to do with continued high unemployment, severe income disparity, the failure of global governance systems owing to a lack of trust in institutions, and the potential for political and social instability as a result. This vision is not divine prophecy; society can intervene on its own behalf. Governments can make sure that the benefits of growth are equitably shared. For this they need the will of their constituents. This will needs role models that guide society toward shared understanding and consensus.

Luxury brands are what people emulate. Luxury brands cannot by themselves fix society's problems. But they should not contribute to them: they should not suggest that the breadless eat brioche while their own crowd sips champagne from glass slippers. They should get away from the image of themselves as purveyors of simple extravagance, excess, glamour, and opulence, and mine the rich culture and intellect that feed the heritage and creativity they advertise. Like a fruit tree, the flowers attract the bees that help it propagate. But it is the fruit, nourished by the soil, which provides nutrition. Without deep roots in the nutrient-rich earth, there are no flowers. And if you harvest all the flowers, there will be no fruit. So, it is not the florid symbols of luxury that make its value, but the unglamorous, hard-won knowledge and skill. It is not the towering, inaccessible treetops that give luxury its strength, but the hidden and porous roots deeply anchored in the ground. A luxury brand can only be revived from the root, not the flower petals that provide a whiff of its scent and a hint of its color. And a luxury brand can only be protected by protecting its entire ecosystem, not just spreading its seed.

From fragmentation and abstraction to knowledgeable communities

Technology is the main driver of the shifting social and business environment. By introducing speed and interconnection, it makes our world more complicated in so many ways. It vastly increases the quantity and complexity of information we have to manage and introduces the new potential for local crises to lead to system-wide epidemics. Because technology has revolutionized the way we gather and convey information, people's expectations and priorities are evolving. The sum total of technological revolution is the fragmentation, abstraction, and interconnection that it creates in society, and the consequent effect these have on how and what we value. Technology allows us to go faster. It gives us the possibility of instant information, instant reaction, and instant results. This overwhelms us and makes our attention span and memory grow shorter. We become passionate about something, then quickly get bored of it and move on to the next new thing, only to excitedly "discover" the first thing again 20 things later. Further, technology organizes knowledge and relationships into systems. It makes everything objective and measurable, accessible even from a long distance. But humans thrive on variety and only truly appreciate things in contrast with other things. So, the ability to go faster makes us yearn to go slower: to take the time to think through an idea, to savor a moment, to appreciate the present and what we have. Since information is not knowledge, the more information and possibilities we have at our disposal, the more we desire to fully understand a particular aspect of a particular thing. And the ability to plug into anything makes us yearn to form a relationship with something reliable, deep, and authentic.

As we adapt to the possibilities of technology, it also provides the solutions to these problems by helping us spread knowledge and organize communities to use that knowledge. In the early days of the Internet, people naively rushed in to establish relationships and do business with unknown partners around the globe. We built networked interactions with little or no safety mechanisms to protect our selves and our entities from trouble that may develop elsewhere. As the Internet grew, so eventually did fear and mistrust as we became aware of how vulnerable our privacy and security were becoming. Revelations about the US National Security Agency gathering intelligence, whether by tapping world leaders' phones or mass harvesting data from the records of cell phone companies, are a testament of just how exposed everyone has become. But the fact that these revelations happened at all, their scale and the access the public has through websites like WikiLeaks also show that the vulnerability works both ways. If institutions can track us, we can track them back. Figure 8.2 illustrates how the spread of information leads to greater accountability and higher levels of engagement, which in turn continues the spread of information. IT first made our individual worlds bigger, like moving to a big city filled with lots of strangers. But now it is shrinking the world down, like a small town where people trust one another because the closeness of their interactions creates a peer pressure that keeps people on the straight and narrow. The Internet once gave anonymity to miscreants. More and more it makes all of us more easily identifiable. It makes it harder to tell untrue stories and cover up inconvenient realities. It pushes people's and organizations' behaviors toward authenticity with their words. It pushes them toward more honest dialogue, which then perpetuates the virtuous cycle.

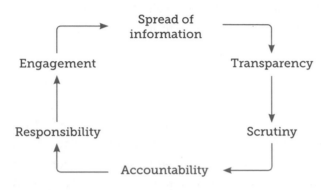

FIGURE 8.2 / The enlightenment cycle

Knowledge used to be contained in books, of which there were limited examples. Even if you had one, you had to know how to read, often in Latin. When Catholic services were held in Latin, priests controlled access to knowledge. When the Church moved its liturgy to the vernacular, it allowed ordinary people to interpret religious doctrine according to their own thinking. This opened the door to the Protestant Reformation, highlighting people's direct relationship with God and changing the role of priests from being the gatekeepers of salvation to being spiritual guides. Faith became more personal, leading to agnosticism and even atheism, and giving people the freedom to focus on spirituality and morality rather than formal doctrine. Interestingly, this brought us back to the age of philosophers and allowed Western and Eastern faiths to converge. One can now be born Episcopalian but choose to live by Buddhist values without declaring themselves to be either one. Thus, wellbeing went from being about salvation in the afterlife to a state of "Zen" in this one.

The democratization of knowledge in the search for wellbeing has paralleled the democratization of wealth in the search for value. When money becomes abstract, the definition of value becomes more fluid. Money was originally struck from gold or silver. When money was a raw material, countries got richer by conquering lands and controlling the distribution of its supply. With the invention of paper currency, money essentially became a promissory note that the holder could, in principle, use to demand gold from a country's reserves. But the gold standard ceased to exist a half century ago. Money is now entirely fiat, with value based simply in the government's commitment to enforce its face value. It is worth only the paper on which it is written, inasmuch as that paper represents a government guarantee. Thanks to technology, money does not even need to be printed anymore. You probably get paid for your work and pay your bills without ever touching actual currency. Digital information is simply attributed from one account to another. Wealth can even be hypothetical. Financial instruments such as shares rise and fall in cash value from minute to minute. In this way, money begets more money. When you have the right knowledge, it can be its own source of value creation. So, if consumers respond to crisis by letting value guide their purchases, with growing knowledge they will start to rely on the ability of their purchase to retain and even grow its value for the future. This is familiar to the world of luxury, as when a particular type of individual uses the sale of an inherited painting or a judiciously assembled collection of jewels, wines, or haute couture as a way to raise funds.

The convergence between the changing possibilities for achieving wellbeing and perpetuating value gives birth to a new type of community with a powerful role for luxury brands. Without the structure of a religious establishment framing people into communities, people use their values to coalesce into self-selecting groups, which is what gives social networks their power. The exchange of information that happens in social media increases our knowledge further and pushes society toward more honesty and responsibility. At the same time, technology creates a worldwide resale market. What we already own is increasingly seen as a source of wealth, provided we buy judiciously. We buy, we get the use of the product we purchased, and then we put it back into the system and recoup the residual value. Forget eBay, online bidders brought in almost $21 million in sales at Christie's in 2013.[8] This is not about money, but about value, which can be interpreted in multiple ways. For some people it may be about the resale value in order to raise funds, for others it may be about limiting the impact on the environment, either by not consuming resources or not generating waste. Notice the value chain that forms when the environmental value for one person translates into resale value for another. This only holds, however, if the product itself does not devalue with use. To buy judiciously we need knowledge. Luxury brands should be the vehicles for this knowledge. Educating the public is a way for them to create shared value, provided that education increases their appreciation for what makes something valuable and not just expensive. Like the role of priests in people's search for wellbeing, luxury brands go from being a gatekeeper to being a guide.

Getting from why to how

The ability of luxury brands to adapt to this new environment is intricately bound up with notions of leadership and stewardship. Luxury brands are the accoutrements of leadership. Luxury brands are also leaders themselves. This makes a potent cocktail with which luxury brands can assure their long-term relevance if they can see themselves as something more than purveyors of expensive goods and services. The 1980s were a time of materialism and many of today's best-known brands went from being hidden treasures to household names during that era. But their success was based less on what they had been doing than on what happened next. With solid brand equity but stuck in old business models and lacking clear vision for their future, they became juicy targets for new corporate owners with more ambitious ideas.

The most successful brands owe their dominant positions to the professional management that took over, infused capital, cleaned up messy licensing and distribution contracts, centralized control of brand image, and brought in talent from other sectors with fresh and current ways of thinking. What emerged was a new vision of a luxury brand that has a homogeneous global presence and complete control of its value chain. The design of every Louis Vuitton, Gucci, or Dior point of sale was coordinated in every city, down to the window displays. Be it in Beverly Hills or Bangkok, you were reassured by the consistency of the brand you were dealing with. By 2000, however, luxury customers and the press were already bemoaning the standardization of luxury; luxury goods were losing their uniqueness, with the same things available everywhere. In response, luxury brands put the accent on personalization of existing products, limited editions, capsule collections, creative collaborations, and stores differentiated for specific locations, collections, or events.

The intent was to enrich a brand experience that uniformity had rendered two-dimensional. But when brands pursue this in a corporate way, they are commoditizing their art. How can a brand have a global presence and still be able to have an intimate conversation with an individual? The answer is to accommodate the fragmentation of society without breaking into a million pieces itself, and accommodate the abstraction of value while maintaining its own value proposition. The individual decides what they value, but the brand decides whether and how to meet their expectations.

The brand defines the experience, but leaves the individual free to shape it and take away the knowledge they are looking for.

In 2014, Moynat designed a case that holds an electric scooter and fits the precise shape of both the scooter and the trunk of the powerful new Jaguar F-type coupe. This complex intellectual inversion shows how a historic brand can dialogue with modernity in a richly symbolic and pragmatically meaningful way. First, the trunk within a trunk shows how Moynat, which came to fame designing trunks that married precisely to the exterior shapes of early automobiles, uses their vision to refashion the relationship between a car and its cargo. Second, designed to carry a scooter seamlessly within a performance car, the trunk is a marriage of several contrasts. On the one hand, the contrasting technologies of automotive engineering and artisanal trunk making and, on the other, the contrasting speeds the individual can use to form their experience. Like yacht and tender, the combination of car and scooter allows you to travel to a destination with all the muscle of modern technology, but then to explore that destination at a human scale and pace. It allows the individual to have the best of both by engaging the contrasting stimuli that allow us to appreciate pleasure. The speed and simplicity each yield their own kind of pleasure. The third pleasure derives from the contrast between the two, and makes the whole experience greater than the sum of its parts. The Moynat trunk, in marrying the shapes of the two vehicles, tops it all off with the additional pleasure of combining these contrasts with grace and beauty. Technology pushes the artistry. The physical and the metaphysical combine.

The same approach can be translated to the all-important retail experience. The Boston Consulting Group's 2014 study of luxury declared that the age of the global retail store is over.[9] The consultancy point out that consumers in Shanghai and Paris have more in common with each other than they do with shoppers in secondary cities in their own countries. Global messaging must have local relevance. These adaptations are more than stylistic. It is not enough to simply pick up on Chinese architectural codes to envelope a French brand vision. Rather, it must be a marriage of values that combines the brand's and the location's cultures, creating a new whole that is more than the sum of its parts. An example of this is the retail approach used by Aesop skincare products. Each store is designed individually in collaboration with a local artist or designer, and interprets the character of the neighborhood through local materials, yet expresses Aesop's personality of "intellectual rigor, vision, and a nod to the whimsical."[10]

Furthermore, adventurous, upwardly mobile, educated, creative, and entrepreneurial professionals are no longer confined to "the big city". Chicago was considered a provincial outpost by venture capitalists on the East and West coasts during the first dotcom boom. By 2013, it was being called an entrepreneurial hotbed, with a fifteenfold increase in startup activity over the previous decade and billions of dollars flowing into the area's universities, technology incubators, and new ventures.[11] As cities like New York, London, Paris, and even San Francisco are increasingly seen as wealthy ghettos, sanitized versions of their former selves stripped of the grit and authenticity that gave life there its texture, a pioneering class is opting for so-called second cities and even small towns from which they remain connected to the world through technology.

This pushes the retail experience to an even greater convergence between real world and virtual, changing the purpose of the store. It is now the point for people to have a physical experience of the brand's metaphysical aspects. The customer is not necessarily there to make a purchase, but certainly to explore the product, ask questions of a live person, and immerse themselves in the brand's complete sensorial and emotional experience. They take this knowledge away with them, regardless of whether they make a purchase right then and there. So, if the retail store is designed to make a sale rather than to dialogue and educate, it is missing the whole point of the person's visit. The future of brick and mortar stores is as a foot on the ground – literally, a pied à terre – for a single retail operation that functions through the cloud. As in a museum, the customer can always choose to purchase their part of the acculturation as they exit through the gift shop, but the store, as such, is there more to build appreciation of and demand for the art.

This shift also confirms that, in an era of high engagement and transparency, everything that a brand does is a form of communication. Communication, then, is just the outward expression of the same culture that determines how a brand operates. In this light, it is instructive to look at the cultural and behavioral associations that luxury brands have been expressing until now.

Private banks, for example, rely on a standard set of images. Bank Muscat's image shows a long, tree-lined road marked "Private," accompanied by the slogan "Exclusivity, because you value it." Swiss Life offer an image of extreme serenity with the reminder that "One can have money and live without having to think about it." ABN AMRO are "Protecting wealth. For generations." Especially those standing together on the stairs of a manor house. And Dexia are "For those who are used to being spoiled," such as by a butler pouring boiling water to warm the ocean while his boss swims alongside the yacht. Only Crédit Agricole remind us that luxury is lived differently, such as by camping in solitude on a mountain peak. More creative brands, such as those in fashion or other lifestyle sectors, might sneer at the fustiness of private banking's vision, but these bankers are themselves luxury customers, so their vision is telling of what the wider luxury universe is saying to itself. Fashion's vapid waifs draped on a designer sofa, pouting either languidly or defiantly at the viewer, is hardly any less of a cliché.

So too luxury hospitality. Since the establishment of Aman Resorts as a successful concept and brand, many others have entered the field of sublimely designed, understated, and sustainable luxury. Some truly share the Aman philosophy of simplicity, while others are more opportunistic, imitating the Aman aesthetic and language to capitalize on their success. Luxury hotels typically position themselves as pampering, soothing, and personalized experiences. The traditional luxury hospitality model is based on exceptional facilities and service. Today's luxury hotels provide the additional layer of mood, like the exclusive intimacy of private homes.

The next stage in this evolution will build on the physical and emotional attributes by participating in the guest's values. Going beyond personalized service, staff and guests no longer relate as categories, but as individuals. The property is no longer a passive venue, but a values-based experience of interactions responding to each guest. As at home, when we receive a guest, the dialogue that results enriches the host and the guest. This means that hospitality is no longer about providing a place to withdraw, but a place to come together – be it in a physical or a philosophical sense – which is the true meaning of hospitality. Viewed in this light, hospitality is not just a simple rest stop, and more about a place to prepare and propel oneself in a positive direction on the journey ahead.

This kind of exchange opens the door to a radically different approach to a luxury company's social responsibility, using its communications to start a conversation and propagate a culture. Social and environmental responsibility are rapidly becoming an expected part of business. Sustainability and CSR reporting are now standard and often a regulatory requirement. Cause marketing has been unmasked as an effort by brands to win market share rather than a meaningful commitment to a cause. Corporate foundations and philanthropic capsule collections offer consumers little beyond a bit of "feel-good" factor in their purchasing. So, rather than trying to please customers with anecdotal evidence and flavor-of-the-month initiatives, the bar will be raised for brands to truly prove the value they bring to society. This will be an important motivator for customers looking to make their consumption more conscientious, as well as for employees looking to do more than make shareholders rich. If these perspectives are not yet universal, neither are they sufficiently rare to make a brand or product stand out. If anything, brands that are not on the bandwagon are singled out for negative differentiation. The product quality hurdles to sustainability are quickly being overcome. Consumers are more easily finding satisfactory, responsible alternatives to the products they seek, so brands must fully integrate their approaches to creating social and business value.

In 2012, the founders of Patagonia, the high-end outerwear brand, changed their company status to that of a B Corporation, or public benefit corporation. This move forever protects the company's practice of allocating a share of their revenues to environmental protection. This placed the company's social responsibility squarely within the core of their activity. Even if Patagonia were one day to become a publicly listed firm, their shareholders would have a clear indication of their philosophy and business model that preserving the environment is essential to their commercial success. In doing so, the owners of Patagonia today are thinking beyond themselves and securing their vision for the future. Patagonia demonstrate how new forms of company structure, such as social enterprises, are cementing the future vision of businesses as responsible and accountable social actors. In fact, this is also the past vision of business as one of creating value by addressing a pressing problem or widely shared need, before that vision was subsumed by production and profit as the ultimate goal. Companies that want to thrive will have to recognize that in a world of abundant products, needs are different and more complicated. And they will have to learn to respond based on a desire broader than their own self-interest.

In conclusion

None of this replaces what luxury already is. It just adds other dimensions. If luxury brands now aim to be socially responsible, this does not mean their customers are prepared to compromise on quality or creativity. If luxury brands are excellent, they must be excellent at everything they do. Today's actions can be tomorrow's heritage if they are sufficiently visionary. The yearning for comfort, beauty, and rarity is innate to the human psyche. There will continue to be customers who look for the kind of luxury we are familiar with today: newly rich and aspiring consumers who link their feeling of success with extravagant icons of conspicuous consumption. But luxury brands must offer new and different manifestations that respond to diversifying desires.

If luxury brands think abstractly about their role, about the purpose of luxury in society, and about their function within that purpose, this opens up new possibilities for creating products that have meaning beyond the familiar stories of heritage, artistry, and craftsmanship. If luxury brands see themselves in a leadership role, this gives new purpose to their communications and gives them new status. Luxury represents an ideal that is physical and metaphysical. Luxury is not just the object but the world in which we can dream of that object; where that object is something positive and resides in a positive context. Gold is precious not because it is shiny, but because it represents purity and nobility. This metaphysical aspect of the material adds to its physical rarity and makes it not just precious but also noble. Its nobility drives the sense of purpose when the craftsperson works on that material, gives it form and function, and transforms it into an object of luxury. Take away the metaphysical aspect of the material and the human purpose, and all you are left with is a pretty object, a bit of metal, a piece of leather, a scrap of fabric. Luxury must give people something to work toward, a positive vision of the future, of work, of consumption, of sustainability, of harmony. In short, a vision of quality of life rather than quantity of wealth. Luxury is often equated to being superfluous, but if it were not valuable, it would not survive. The key is to mine this value in a way that reinforces rather than depletes it. These actions become a form of reinvestment that ensures continuous returns over the long term.

Luxury firms have a vested interest in adopting a shared value model. Their character accounts for a larger part of their reputation than their products. Yet the spread of luxury makes it difficult to offer value propositions that are substantively different from those of competitors. Aspiration gives luxury brands the power to lead, and real luxury is about leadership. Is it enough for luxury brands to be leaders of the status quo? Luxury brands have the potential and raw material to incite innovation and progress toward wellbeing. Refocusing aspiration from affiliation with a product to affiliation with a purpose turns luxury consumption from a conspicuous act into an intelligent act. Realizing shared value emanates from an honest assessment of the brand's relationships with its stakeholders all along the value chain. Shared value methods leverage the power of branding and communications to reach the individual and earn their buy-in on a personal level. The key to creating shared value is to build confidence in society by empowering individuals and helping them be responsible for their actions.

Leadership is ultimately about creating cultures. In a complicated, interconnected world, leadership is about helping people understand and respond appropriately to rapidly changing dynamics. This means addressing complex challenges in a way that creates shared value among a broad range of stakeholders. Shared value nourishes the firm by nourishing its environment. Shared value makes brands complete, unique, and inimitable. Luxury brands, as potent cultural leaders, are uniquely placed to do this through their visibility, their magnetism, and their ability to influence what people aspire to and desire. Shared value takes luxury brands from desirable to indispensable.

Notes

1   Cannarella, J. and Spechler, J. (2014) "Epidemiological modeling of online social network dynamics." Princeton University. January 17.

2   McCarthy, J. (2014) "Emerging brands lack the heritage needed for luxury status." *Luxury Daily*, January 16.

3   WIN/Gallup (2013) *End of Year 2013: Giving the World a Voice for the 37th Time*. WIN/Gallup International Association, December 30.

4   Johansson, A., Guillemette, Y., Mutin, F. et al. (2012) *Looking to 2060: Long-Term Global Growth Prospects: A Going for Growth Report*. OECD Economic Policy Papers, No. 3. OECD Publishing.

5   Hurun Report (2014) "Hurun Report Chinese Luxury Consumer Survey 2014". January 16.

6   Wolf, M. (2014) "Failing elites threaten our future". *Financial Times*, January 14.

7   World Economic Forum (2014) *Global Risks 2014: Ninth Edition*. WEF.

8   Brooker, K. (2014) "The new auction action." *Newsweek*, January 24.

9   Ahtan, O., Achille, A., Bellaïche J.-M, et al. (2014) *Shock of the New Chic: Dealing with New Complexity in the Business of Luxury*. The Boston Consulting Group, January 30.

10   www.aesop.com/uk/about_aesop.

11   Deeb, G. (2013) "Chicago's startup scene is on fire." *Forbes*, November 19.

Background reading

Arendt, H. (1998) *The Human Condition*, 2nd edn. University of Chicago Press.

Arthur W. Page Society (2007) *The Authentic Enterprise. An Arthur W. Page Society Report*. Arthur W. Page Society.

Berne, E. (1964) *Games People Play: The Psychology of Human Relationships*. Penguin Books.

Bonini, S., Court, D. and Marchi, A. (2009) "Rebuilding corporate reputations." *McKinsey Quarterly*, 3: 75–83.

Bryant, J. (2009) *Love Leadership: The New Way to Lead in a Fear-Based World*. Jossey-Bass.

BSR (2010) *Redefining Leadership*, BSR Report.

Cassidy, J. (2010) "What good is Wall Street." *The New Yorker*, November 29.

Farzad, R. (2013) "This market is going higher, warns Jeremy Grantham." *Business Week*, November 20.

Ferguson, N. (2006) *The War of the World: Twentieth-Century Conflict and the Descent of the West*. Penguin Press.

Foley, M. (2011) *The Age of Absurdity: Why Modern Life Makes it Hard to be Happy*. Simon & Schuster.

Gabler, N. (2000) *Life: The Movie: How Entertainment Conquered Reality*. Vintage.

Gertner, J. (2010) "The rise and fall of GDP." *The New York Times*, May 10.

Hébel, P. (2013) *La Révolte des Moutons: Les Consommateurs au Pouvoir*. Éditions Autrement.

Jung, C.G. (2002) *The Undiscovered Self*. Routledge.

Lelièvre, M.-D. (2010) *Saint Laurent, Mauvais Garçon*. Flammarion.

Machiavelli (1947) *The Prince* (trans. Bergen, T.). Appleton-Century.

McKibbin, R. (2010) "Nothing to do with the economy." *London Review of Books*, November 23.

Marx, K. and Engels, F. (2002) *The Communist Manifesto* (trans. Moore, S.). Penguin Books.

Michaud, Y. (2013) *Le Nouveau Luxe: Expériences, Arrogance, Authenticité*. Éditions Stock.

Plato (2007) *The Republic*. Penguin Books.

Rousseau, J.-J. (2004) *The Social Contract* (trans. Cranston, M.). Penguin Books.

Samans, R., Schwab, K. and Malloch-Brown, M. (2011) "Running the world, after the crash." *Foreign Policy*, 184: 80–3.

Seidman, D. (2007) *How: Why HOW We Do Anything Means Everything... in Business (and in Life)*. Wiley & Sons.

Senior, J. (2006) "Can't get no satisfaction." *New York Magazine*, November 26.

Vaynerchuk, G. (2011) *The Thank You Economy*. Harper Business.

Watson, B. (tr.) (2007) *The Analects of Confucious*. Columbia University Press.

Yalom, I. (1980) *Existential Psychotherapy*. Basic Books.

Index

Bold page numbers indicate a more extensive discussion of the topic

Printed and bound in Great Britain by
CPI Group (UK) Ltd, Croydon, CR0 4YY